to my Turquoise Table queen,

Start at chapter 4 — that's
the fly-fishing chapter.

Happy Beaming!
Megan Willome

THE JOY OF POETRY

how to keep, save & make your life with poems

megan willome

masters in fine living series

ts T. S. Poetry Press • New York

T. S. Poetry Press
Briarcliff, New York
Tspoetry.com
© 2016 by Megan Willome

Cover image by Pai-Shi Lee.
www.facebook.com/SomewhereInLife

ISBN 978-1-943120-14-7

Library of Congress Cataloging-in-Publication Data:
Willome, Megan
    [Nonfiction.]
    The Joy of Poetry/Megan Willome
    ISBN 978-1-943120-14-7
    Library of Congress Control Number: 2016935923

The Joy of Poetry
is available on Amazon.com

for Merry Nell

Table of Contents

1

As Much as She Could Carry

Collecting Poetry

The first poem I ever published was due to the efforts of my mother, Merry Nell Drummond. I was 13 at the time and had an assignment to rewrite "The Night Before Christmas." I wrote about a man helping his neighbor and re-titled it "A Visit of Charity." I'm not sure how my poem ended up on the front page of our town's weekly newspaper, the *Westlake Picayune*, but I'm pretty sure my mother had something to do with it.

I had no idea that more than 30 years later I'd still be writing poetry. I didn't know I'd have scrapbooks of collected poetry, a new one for each new year. I didn't know I'd read at least one poem every day. I didn't know I'd journal about poems that were especially meaningful or especially clever. I certainly didn't know I'd write about poetry in a book. But if I had written a letter to my 13-year-old self with the benefit of hindsight, it would have said, "Stick with poetry. You'll need it."

My Christmas poem was published in 1984, the first time my mother's cancer came back. She was originally diagnosed with breast cancer in 1981, when she was 35. Three years later the cancer returned in her cervical vertebrae. It was as if her neck suddenly broke. When the radiologist saw her scans, he fell to his knees and said out loud, "Oh, my God." Her oncologist thought with radiation and a hysterectomy, he could buy her another year or two; the radiologist thought six months was a more accurate prediction. After undergoing the recommended treatment she went on, happy and healthy and apparently cancer-free for the next 23 years.

But she wasn't cancer-free. She had a lovely pause. During that pause she saw me and my brother graduate from high school and then college. He finished law school. She welcomed five grandbabies into the world. But the cancer reappeared in 2007 in her liver. Tests revealed it was the original breast cancer in a new location.

When cancer moves to the liver, it's fatal. Patients don't qualify for a liver transplant because once the cancer finds that pathway, it will find it again. Her treatment plan included alternating courses of hormone therapy and chemotherapy. Later, radiation therapy would be added. During her last three years, I began writing poems in earnest for the first time in a couple of decades.

After the publication of my Christmas poem I continued to write poetry in high school, when it was assigned, but I gave it up in college. For years I focused on marriage and children, not poetry. When I went back to work as a writer at a city magazine, I started reading a poem a day. It was my personal writing ritual—a poem from *The Writer's Almanac* and a pot of tea kept the words flowing. But until my mother's cancer returned, I only wrote a poem when the mood struck, and it didn't strike often. With the change in her health status, I needed the kind of sustenance I could store. I needed a mouse named Frederick.

Published in 1967, *Frederick,* by Leo Lionni, was a Caldecott Honor Book featuring a mouse who is also a poet. While the other mice gather food during harvest time, Frederick gathers sun and colors and words, which he shares with his fellow mice in their stone den during the winter. When the mice are cold and depressed, having exhausted their store of nuts, they ask Frederick for his supplies. He gives them a poem about seasons. All these years later, the book still has a fine message: We need words during dark days.

Let's imagine our poet Frederick wrote more than the one rather sweet rhyming poem featured in the book. What if he wrote a silly one all the mouse children would memorize (and their parents would wish they'd forget)? What if he wrote a couple of really weird ones? Might dear Frederick write a sexy poem to whisper in the evening to his favorite lady mouse? Or a ghost poem about a headless squirrel who comes looking for hidden nuts? Maybe Frederick might write a monster poem, just for fun.

Monsters

furry,
fluffy,
feared.

scaly,
slimy,
seen.

ghostly,
gassy,
gone.

pointed,

purple,
possible.

monsters,
under your bed,
in your closet,
waiting and watching.

—*Katherine E. McGhee*

Although the book ends with all the mice complimenting Frederick on his poetry, perhaps when spring finally arrives, each of them will gather their own words, along with berries and seeds. Maybe the next time winter comes, there will be more words from more mice to share.

Comparing winter to cancer is an obvious metaphor, but it is useful. In my mother's story, her cancer ebbed and flowed from 1981 to 2010. Some seasons were longer and more intense than others. Hers ended in spring. And during the late winter of her cancer I was Frederick, writing poems, 72 in all. This book contains some of those, as well as poems by others I discovered along the way, in every season. Some of them came to me after she was gone.

Don't expect a trove of maudlin poems. I needed variety. I needed every type of poem Frederick ever considered writing, along with poetry written by contemporary poets like Mary Oliver and Billy Collins, previous-generation poets like Sara Teasdale and Shakespeare, and a host of poets I'd never heard of, like Ruth Mowry, until, through serendipity, I found them.

The earth's economy

Just when I thought the day
had nothing left to give,
when heat was ladled across
the shallow dry plate

of the nation, working or not, alive
or not, my country
road home from work
an affair of sour radio news and roadkill —

the furred skunk, possum, cat,
squirrel, raccoon, in the
special economy of the outward-
facing nose, lost in final scent,

the surrendered open mouth,
forehead pressed back in frozen
tragedy, tension gone, time done,
appetite dissolving into skull —

I find myself at the kitchen counter
in a different Americana, tearing
kale ruffles from their spines
for a chilled supper of greens with lemon

and oil, Dijon, garlic, cucumber —
live, wet and impossibly cool from the

earth garden just outside the door,
where the farmer's wife one hundred

years ago also opened her apron
like a cradle, gingerly receiving
into thin billowing cotton pockets
as much as she could carry

as much as she could carry

—*Ruth Mowry*

This poem surprised me like finding an unexpected nut in January. Often "when I thought the day/had nothing left to give" I'd read a poem, and everything would change. I love that roadkill (which I loathe) and kale (which I love) both appear in this poem. I am neither the woman in the kitchen, tearing kale, nor the farmer's wife, opening "her apron/like a cradle." I am the one "gingerly receiving" the gifts from the poem as it moves from the hard pungency of death to the joy of unexpected bounty. How much?

As much as I could carry. As much as I could carry.

2

Every Day Uncrossed

Everyday Poetry

In 2008, our family—my husband John, our son and daughter, and myself—spent the week after Christmas in Winter Park, Colorado, along with John's parents, his siblings, and their families. They all went downhill skiing, and I snowshoed with my father-in-law, the only other person in the family who enjoys slower snow activities.

I talked to my mother every day of that vacation as she began what turned out to be a very toxic round of chemo. The word "positive" does not even approach Mom's attitude toward cancer. In an email to her friends and supporters, she used words like *conquerors* and *warriors*, adding, "Another term we like is *champions* because victory over adversity is implied. Most of us are not too keen about the term *survivor* because it has a connotation of *victim*," she wrote.

I had an aversion to the very words she loved. Was it possible to be a *conqueror*, a *champion*, when the end was not in doubt?

On the first day of the new year, 2009, I sat on the porch of the cabin where we were staying, with a mug of hot tea, and wrote this haiku.

Winter Sunrise

orange and pink rises
above our snowy cabin
brighter than cancer

Later my father-in-law and I snowshoed around Monarch Lake, and it was as pretty a winter day as I've ever seen in that part of Colorado. Every evergreen was covered with powdery snow, and every naked branch sparkled with icicles. I spent the entire day thinking about my mother, knowing that when we returned to Texas, I'd accompany her to more chemo appointments, and I'd write more poems—a lot of them not as hopeful as this one. But writing this one literally changed my attitude.

In an interview with poet Patty Paine at *Tweetspeak Poetry*, Maureen Doallas writes, "Paine confides that 'poetry, the reading and the writing of it, has saved my life.'" Poetry did the same for me during my mother's last three years, through both reading and writing it.

But most people, even most writers, aren't like me. A lot are like my friend Nancy Franson—they're afraid of poetry. Nancy even used the word *askeered* and added that she battled "poetry demons," the kind that spring up in classrooms where poetry is treated like an equation to be solved.

Are you askeered of poetry? Do you battle poetry demons? Do you feel shut out of the poetry party—as if through a window, there are people dressed up, drinking champagne and dancing away the old year, and there you are, nose pressed against the glass, wondering why you haven't been invited? Consider this book an invitation.

Instead of starting with a New Year's party, let's make our first foray into poetry by way of the farmer's market. There are people carrying satchels, standing in raggedy lines with sweaty cash, and what on earth is that? Some variety of squash, or a sestina? Everyone else seems to know the differences between each type of tomato and how to cook with each one, and all I want is some *fresh* tomatoes, a nice little poem.

The Internet can be a giant farmer's market for poetry with lots of free samples. Day after day, week after week, year after year, I learn what I like by trying new things.

I might fall in love with a pomegranate—say, John Berryman, who wrote some strange stuff. Pomegranates are delicious, but they're a lot of work to peel, and they turn my hands pink in the process. Some days I don't want to do the work Berryman requires, although his words are usually enticing. Other days I want fresh-picked blackberries—a little Mary Oliver, who has written poems about blackberries, which are actually about wildness rather than the joys of fruit.

Poetry doesn't need a lot of fanfare. It's like a fingerling potato, growing quietly in a dark space. Dig it up, saute it in a little olive oil, give it a chance.

So many people are afraid to try. They've been taught that poetry is hard, that it has secret meanings, or that they're supposed to *ooh* and *ahh* over every word. Their paradigm is sitting in a classroom, reading something they don't understand, while the teacher explains in words too dull to repeat why this poem is Great.

Some poems are truly great and some, though they may be great, remain obscure. The key is exposure. We can't say we don't like a food if we've never tried it, and we won't know whether we like a poet until we taste his or her words. Maybe a few tastes.

Tweetspeak Poetry has introduced me to more poets and poems than I can count. (Some of my favorites show up in the comment section.) I spend a small bit of cash and subscribe to *Every Day Poems*, *Tweetspeak's* weekday delivery via email of a hand-selected poem, paired with beautiful art and organized around a monthly theme. Although I try everything the service offers, I don't love every poem—no one says I have to.

Here are some of my recent reactions to selections from *Every Day Poems*:

1) What does that word mean? Oh, now the poem makes more sense. I'm glad I looked that up. I can't imagine a more perfect word.

2) Hmm. It's fine, I guess. Oh, look who wrote it. She's good. Let me read it again. Oh, wow—it's a sonnet. Read it a third time. Well done!

3) This explains my entire life. Print it. Read it aloud while pacing. Save it in my poetry scrapbook. Read it one more time, then put it away and reluctantly get to work.

4) Not. For. Me.

5) Clever. I like how she wove some history in with her moral dilemma. Makes me think of *Charlotte's Web*. What was the big pig's name at the fair?

6) I love poems with humor. This is the first time I've smiled all day.

7) Sigh. So true.

8) Where's my poetry journal? So much to write about in this one.

9) Meh. Seems like someone woke up and said, "On this hallowed day I shall compose a poem, and it wilt be praised by poets throughout the land, though none shall agree what it means." Next.

10) I don't get the beginning, but that image at the end—amazing. I've never heard it said better.

11) Oh, I know this one. It gets better every time I read it.

12) I'll never see yellow the same way again.

Most of these observations aren't long. Other than looking up one word in the dictionary, I didn't do any sleuthing, didn't read any literary criticism, didn't trace any allusions. I simply read the poem and gave it a thumbs up or down based on my gut reaction.

Is that bad? Am I short-changing the poet? Possibly. But at least I'm reading. Because I never know when I'll find the secret something I need to get through the day, in a handful of oddly-spaced words.

Ever since that New Year's when I was away from my mother, January 1 has become a time of reckoning for me. I don't do resolutions, but I do pause and consider where I've been and where I might be going.

Dana Gioia is a poet who believes poetry does the most good when it gets out of the literary world and stretches its legs —maybe at a farmer's market, maybe around a mountain lake, maybe even in an infusion room.

New Year's

Let other mornings honor the miraculous.
Eternity has festivals enough.
This is the feast of our mortality,
The most mundane and human holiday.

On other days we misinterpret time,
Pretending that we live the present moment.
But can this blur, this smudgy in-between,
This tiny fissure where the future drips

Into the past, this flyspeck we call now
Be our true habitat? The present is
The leaky palm of water that we skim
From the swift, silent river slipping by.

The new year always brings us what we want
Simply by bringing us along—to see

A calendar with every day uncrossed,
A field of snow without a single footprint.

—*Dana Gioia*

There is no feeling more grand than leaving a snowshoe print in a field of pristine snow. Each year when I hang a new calendar "with every day uncrossed," no matter what may have happened in the previous 12 months, I can't help but hope the new year might bring joy, most likely through poetry, the one thing that can meet me when nothing else can.

3

Reeking of Sunshine

Symbols in Poetry

After returning from our Colorado vacation, I resumed my practice of making a day trip for my mother's chemotherapy appointments. I was angry during the entire hour-and-a-half drive to Austin, and after watching her suffer cheerfully for several hours, I was angry the entire hour-and-a-half drive home.

It took me a long time to title this poem. Then I remembered that when Mom successfully ran for Student Assembly at the University of Texas at Austin, her campaign slogan was "There's Sunshine Ahead," which should double as her lifelong philosophy.

There's Sunshine Ahead

I drive to chemo, mad
that Mom's still taking it. Park. Climb the stairs
to the infusion room at the top of the building.

Her cheery voice guides me to her chair,
where her face has aged ten years in three weeks,
like she's been in the sun too long.

She settles herself right in the middle of everything

spreading sunshine in January. When she spies me
she beams.

Everyone wants to revolve around her, like the young
woman who hugs her, offers to bake brownies
(marijuana-laced). Mom politely declines.

A former patient drops by to visit
as if she had a quick appointment at the tanning salon.
They chat with the ladies hooked up on either side
    of Mom.

When they hear her story of 28 years
with this doctor, this disease,
their eyes widen like they just saw the light.

My rage crumples under her warmth. I fetch
ice chips that melt instantly in her hot little mouth.
Her feet are cold, so I tuck her in with a yellow

crocheted blanket, a gift from a friend who wants
to wrap her in sunshine.
When she finishes the day's dose,

we exit and the room is thrown off as if
its sun were swept away,
leaving behind only winter and cancer.

When a friend sent me an email with the subject line "poetry &
pain," one of those national tragedies had happened, and the

Internet was again full of writers writing—offering explanations and links to charitable organizations. When a natural disaster, or a personal one, hits, we crave information. We want five-step plans for how to avoid the same outcome next time. But facts lead to analysis, which can give way to blame. At such times instead of prose, I need poetry. Like Stuart Kestenbaum's "Prayer for Joy."

First, consider the title. What do you think the poem is going to be about? Something religious? Something profound? Something from Hallmark? Instead, the poet directs us to alphabet soup.

Prayer for Joy

What was it we wanted
to say anyhow, like today
when there were all the letters
in my alphabet soup and suddenly
the 'j' rises to the surface.
The 'j', a letter that might be
great for Scrabble, but not really
used for much else, unless
we need to jump for joy,
and then all of a sudden
it's there and ready to
help us soar and to open up
our hearts at the same time,
this simple line with a curved bottom,
an upside down cane that helps
us walk in a new way into this

forest of language, where all the letters
are beginning to speak,
finding each other in just
the right combination
to be understood.

—*Stuart Kestenbaum*

What shall we do with the letter *j*? More importantly, what shall we do with the heavy word *joy*?

In some ways the letter *j* in the poem is a symbol for joy itself, "great for Scrabble, but not really/used for much else, unless." Unless what? "unless/we need to jump for joy." Who jumps for joy, other than a child? Other than my mother, who practically jumped out of her chair with glee when I showed up at her appointment. If I had been served a bowl of alphabet soup that day, I would have been looking for a *d*, as in dig-a-hole-and-disappear.

But sometimes we need that *j*, that joy, to be there "ready to/help us soar and to open up/our hearts at the same time." Maybe what I needed was not a hidey-hole but a sudden joy jump. If only I could have linked emotional jumper cables from Mom to me.

I love how the poet describes the letter *j* as "an upside down cane." I'll never forget that image. A cane is something we lean upon when we begin to weaken. I've never thought of the letter *j* as "this simple line with a curved bottom." That's all joy needs to be. Simple, yet curved. It can swerve away from reality into a small smile.

Attending those chemotherapy sessions with my mother as we visited with nurses and patients and later, when I read to her, allowed us, despite the hard reality, to "walk in a new way into this/forest of language." Appointment by appointment, somehow we found "each other in just/the right combination/to be understood."

The yellow crocheted blanket I mention in my poem was a gift from my mother-in-law, who taught my daughter to crochet. A year later, my daughter made Mom a yellow scarf. It turned out a little short because although she did measure from fingertip to fingertip, as my mother-in-law taught her, she was only 10 years old, and her arms didn't reach far. Mom immediately put it on and told everyone her granddaughter made it.

Yellow was not my mother's favorite color—red was—but yellow was a force in her life. Maybe it goes back to her wedding. My parents were married at St. Luke's on the Lake Episcopal Church in Austin, in a sanctuary with windows instead of walls, on a cliff overlooking a lake. The ceremony took place at sunset, and the bridesmaids wore pink, peach, and yellow to match the view outside. For as long as I can remember, Dad sent Mom yellow roses for every anniversary and special occasion. It seems yellow had special meaning for her, but I never asked what it symbolized in her life.

Author John Green, popular writer of young adult fiction, addressed the subject of symbols in a Q&A on his website about his novel *Paper Towns*. Green said, "And this is very important to remember when reading or writing or painting or talking or whatever: You are never, ever choosing whether to use symbols.

You are choosing which symbols to use."

We're all familiar with images representing something more than the thing itself. Apple pie? America! Pumpkins? Harvest! Stars? Wish! I believe with all my heart that the folks at the Texas Education Agency named the new standardized test STAAR so teachers could make posters with stars on them and pithy slogans like "Reach for the STAARs."

Many people who hate poetry say they don't like it because it isn't literal. When I put out a call on Facebook to ask those who hate poetry to tell me why, I received this common complaint: "It's annoying and I don't understand it. I'm just a literal gal I guess. Why not just say what you mean, ya know."

When I read that comment, I thought of the Amelia Bedelia books, Peggy Parish's series of children's books about Amelia Bedelia, the kooky maid who, when told to dust the furniture, literally pours dust on the furniture. She salvages every disaster by baking a delicious cake or pie at the end of each story.

When it comes to poetry, we can't approach it like Amelia Bedelia. There will be symbols, and they're not as mysterious as we've been led to believe. There will be similes and metaphors, too.

Most of us covered these terms in middle school. What is a simile? A comparison using "like" or "as." What is a metaphor? The other one.

A simile says straight out that a comparison is being made: "My love is like a red, red rose," from a poem by Robert Burns. A metaphor requires a little more work: "My love is a red, red rose." A symbol would be the red rose all by itself with no explanation, like in the opening to the movie *Beauty and the Beast*. Or the letter *j* carrying the heavy weight of joy in alphabet soup.

The reason poets use these tools is because they can make things easier to understand. "Just say what you mean" works fine for an essay or nonfiction, but it can feel flat.

For example, I could write, "My husband loves Baylor University football." That's exactly what I mean. It's literally true. It's also a boring sentence. Or I might write, "If I could only bring four things that describe John, they would all be Baylor football T-shirts." If I were writing a poem, I could show each T-shirt, how the ones from the bad ole days are ragged because those get worn to do the lawn, and the ones from the good years are new and kept looking crisp so they can be worn as good luck charms on game day. The poetic way is still literal but much more interesting.

Here's a literal poem about finding a seashell in the washing machine. It also uses that seashell as a symbol of grief. Mom loved shells. While I was growing up, we went to South Padre Island, at the tip of Texas, for nearly every summer vacation. One year I saved the shells I combed from the beach and bought a ceramic display dish at the local Hallmark store. I put the shells in the curved hollows of the dish and gave it to my mother for her birthday. She's been gone for six years. That dish and those shells are still displayed in her bathroom.

Shell

I found it in the wash, the orange
shell I picked up on the beach
that last time. One of my girls—
the one named after you—

must have found it in my room
and wanted it. Clean calcareous
curve, a palm open to nothing,
reeking of sunshine

and your death. For years
I didn't know what to do with it.
You would have liked
this story: how a child

slips grief into a careless pocket.
Breaks it to pieces. Lets it go.

—*Harriet Brown*

I love the phrase "reeking of sunshine." I would never have thought to link those two words. *Reek* sounds like it should go with garbage, and *sunshine* sounds like it should be displayed in a kindergarten classroom. But when Mom spread joy through the infusion lab, I'd say she was "reeking of sunshine."

Whatever meaning yellow may or may not have had before her cancer, during her last years I think of it as her fighting color, the one she draped herself in with that crocheted blanket and later with my daughter's scarf.

My friend in Connecticut hates winter, and when March came and there was still snow outside her door, she boldly put an artificial forsythia wreath on her door, as if to announce to winter that its days were numbered. She added a hashtag to her photo, #fightbackwithyellow. Maybe that's what my mother was doing, fighting back with a color.

Now I crave yellow. After my son went away to college, I remade his room into a guest room and picked out a new daffodil yellow sheet set. When I put it on the double bed, I blanched. Yellow is so, well, yellow. It needed a little softening, so I bought a white comforter and pale blue pillows. Sometimes I sleep in there. When I pull back the covers, the room is all sun.

4

The Wing of Her Hand

Poetry Buddies

Before my mother got really sick, our family took a vacation with my parents to Creede, Colorado. They went every September, leaving around Labor Day, which was near their wedding anniversary. Since autumn comes early at 8,854 feet above sea level, they always arrived in time to see the aspens turn gold. Mom got rather giddy over aspens. It was a testimony to how much she loved us that she agreed to go in August and miss the turning of the trees.

What she really loved to do in Creede was fly-fish. She didn't discover fly-fishing until later in life, but it gave her so much joy. I should not have been surprised. Fishing is a family thing.

Mom's first fishing buddy—using not a fly rod but a spinning one—was her dad, who died of cancer when she was 16. They fished for trout in South Texas reservoirs, nowhere near mountain streams. She didn't even remember fishing with him until 50 years later, when my parents went fishing in Colorado with friends.

"Fifteen minutes in she knew she had done this before," Dad wrote. "She was surprised. She had seldom been overpowered with a feeling this strong. The kicker was that she caught 12 very nice-sized rainbows that morning."

Those friends gently guided my parents toward fly-fishing.

Soon they were fishing with Mom's sister and her husband, avid fly-fishers who live in Wyoming, where fly-fishing should be a requirement for residency. The last years of Mom's life involved a lot of catch and release, with my dad, her fishing buddy, at her side.

Fly-fishing and poetry go together. Seth Haines wrote at *Tweetspeak* about how the two interacted for him during a season of medical madness. He recalled the words of his fly-fishing mentor:

> *Back; forward; back; forward; release. Don't waste any energy. The fly rod is an extension of you.*
>
> I've been unable to find creative words in the last few weeks. I have struggled to find time to read poetry, much less write it. Time evades. Words evade.
>
> *Back; forward; back; forward; release. Don't waste any energy. The fly rod is an extension of you.*
>
> With practice, I transfer the cares of the world through the fly line, scatter them across the river waters and let them sink with my sow bug. I consider the art of angling, that by graceful repetition, by easy and patient strokes, one can find an inner quiet not often afforded in today's world.

Inner quiet is available at the end of a fly line in a cool river. It can also hide in a poem. But poems and trout are both slippery creatures. If you don't know how to catch one, seek out a mentor or at least a buddy—especially if you're new to poetry.

My poetry buddy was Nancy Franson.

I wasn't looking for a poetry buddy any more than my mother was looking to convert to fly-fishing. Both of us have friends to blame. I accuse LW Lindquist, Director of Many Things at *Tweetspeak* and the official Darer-in-Chief, who sent me an email in June 2013, asking if Nancy and I might be interested in reading a poem a day and posting short articles about our poetry journey.

Nancy and I met at a writer's retreat. I took the poetry workshop, and she took the creative nonfiction class. The next year we both took the fiction workshop. The leader, Jeffrey Overstreet, used poetry to teach fiction, perhaps because his wife, Anne M. Doe Overstreet, is a poet. Nancy and I should've seen it as a sign that poetry was going to be a greater part of our lives.

I asked Nancy why she thought *Tweetspeak* dared her. "I suspect that my comments about being afraid of poetry had something to do with it. A feeling I had missed out on something along the way, like not having been invited to a cool kids' sleepover. Or something," she wrote.

A lot of writers feel like Nancy—they should like poetry, but they don't. Maybe they need a buddy to accompany them as they fish for poems.

In addition to reading and discussing the daily offering from *Every Day Poems*, Nancy and I also sent each other poems lurking behind Internet rocks. If we didn't like a poem, we said so. If the poet lost us, we admitted it. Sometimes one of us would say, "Here, try it again with this fly."

At the end of our dare, which lasted a little longer than a summer, these were Nancy's conclusions:

- Poetry may be mysterious, but it's not dangerous

- Poetry is probably best taught by someone who loves it

- Poetry may not be a subject to be learned at all but rather a conversation, a call-and-response

- The best way to get comfortable with poetry is by reading poetry

- The folks at *Tweetspeak* really do care about having fun and helping people become who they really are

- There is probably not a man, woman or child who couldn't benefit from having a little more poetry in their lives—or a poetry buddy

I still enjoy discussing poetry with a buddy. The year after Nancy and I dared, I dared again with Laura Lynn Brown. This new dare encouraged us to choose one poet to read for an entire month. It actually took us four months to finish Kevin Young's *Book of Hours*, and I wouldn't trade a single day. The poems were about the death of Young's father and the birth of his son. Grief and joy.

Laura already loved poetry. She reads and writes it. So, instead of doing a dare with a novice (Nancy), I was doing a dare with a fan (Laura). Nancy brought enthusiasm and angst and wonderful questions. Laura brought subtlety, novelty, wisdom. A musician herself, Laura compared Young's alliterations to jazz riffs, as if he said to himself, "Hey, let's try this." She noticed things I didn't. She made me a better poetry reader.

After *Every Day Poems* featured the following poem, I discussed it via email with L.L. Barkat, who is not my poetry buddy but the Queen Mother of All Things Poetic.

Mare Draws Her Lover Fishing at Dusk

As dark begins to dissolve the body—
the crown of his head, the belly's swell, the ankle—
I watch him sleep, recall how he settled back
on his heels just hours ago, sent a line keening
swift and precise over the lake. Everyone knows
a cast is not a question of strength so much
as a relinquishing, that the line's release
is an extension from the wrist to the lunge
and snap of a Cutthroat Trout. I sketch in the ribbed
trunk of a cottonwood, label it *Populus trichocarpa*.
Something of what the eye took in is translated
to joint and grip of finger, until ink gives back
the crumbled snag of bark, the silver-sided leaf
dipping like a fish through the evening air.
The wing of his hand is the last thing to go.

—*Anne M. Doe Overstreet*

"An ode to fly-fishing, perhaps?" I wrote. I knew there was more to the poem, but those were the lines that drew me.

For L.L., the poem wasn't about fish. "Now, writing this, I am struck by the word *lines* in the poem and in fact am more convinced than ever that the piece is about poets as much as it is about Mare's lover. Or maybe the poem is about the reader. After all, who does the poet catch with her line, but you and me, while we are unsuspecting? And who does the poet draw, but us, sleeping? When we finally wake, we become the trout, caught and compelled," she wrote.

I wrote back, "A good poem does that—offers multiple gifts upon multiple readings."

Neither L.L. nor I came up with an almighty answer to what the poem means. Neither of us asked Overstreet what she had in mind when she wrote it. Maybe she would emphasize the mare in the title. I re-read the poem to see if casting out my line again might yield a different catch. I'm still overcome by the fishing imagery. Some of my fly-fishing family members live in Jackson Hole, Wyoming, and I was surprised to see cottonwoods there. So now I'm picturing the Snake River as the setting.

There seems to be something in the poem about letting go, about "relinquishing," both in the casting of the line and in the ink creating an image and even in the sleeping. I guess art and fishing have similarities, for the leaf is caught as surely as the fish. Both emerge from "the wing of his hand."

I met L.L. at a poetry workshop taught by Julia Kasdorf. In one exercise, Kasdorf gave us a psalm fragment and asked us to write a poem from it. Mine read, "He catches the helpless and drags them off in his net." I may not be able to fly-fish, but the word *net* made me try my hand at a poem about fly-fishing.

Cutthroat

Dad plans all day for what will be a one-hour trip,

tying flies
gathering vest, hat, waders, net.

We drive our gear down the mountainside
to fish this Wild and Scenic River,
the Rio Grande.

"Where's your pole?" Dad asks.
I hold up a bamboo pole (5 bucks at the gas station).
He frowns. "I'll go help your mother."

Fly-fishing is the only time she is quiet.
Dad arranges everything just so,
just the way she likes it.

The air is cool, but not
the midday sun. Mosquitoes
everywhere.

Me and my cheap pole can't fish and I can't
care as I stand in the freezing river, watch Mom
watch the water.

Dad watches her
cast her line despite the tumor deep in her eye
turning the waves sepia.

Still she is the first to spy
the cutthroat trout
darting right toward Dad.

He sets the hook. Keeps
the tension. Extends the net.
"Get the camera!" he yells.

I drop my pole, paw through Orvis bags but
no camera.
Mom quotes the psalm

as if her Bible were open
beside the riverbank:
He catches the helpless and drags them off in his net.

Dad returns the trout to its home.
He will load up his flies again
but she will not. The Good Lord

will scoop her up
after this tumor connects with the others,
forms a net.

When Dad returns
he will catch another cutthroat.
Snap a photo. Let it go.

Since then my dad has been fly-fishing in New Mexico, Colorado, and "damn near every creek in Wyoming" but with other buddies. He eventually went back to Creede to fly-fish with the couple who first introduced Mom to its joys. I asked him if he thought going back would be hard.

"Every day is hard," he said, so he went. The photo he sent

of himself holding a Colorado cutthroat before he released it back into the wild was the inspiration for my poem.

Like fly-fishing, poetry takes patience. It forces us to travel to obscure streams in all weathers, at dusk and at dawn. We need all five of our senses and any others laying around to serve as flies to catch the words that do not want to be caught. And when an elusive trout finds its way to where we wait, we need to snatch a picture. Sketch it fast. If possible, write the tale. Because it demands to be released.

I have not been back to Creede, but my desire lines run right north. I think about Creede every time I turn on my computer because my screensaver is a photograph I took of the San Juan mountain range. Before she died, Mom drew a picture of those mountains for my daughter, capturing their beauty. Above them soar small birds.

4 (from "Bird On the Mountain")

Don't flee from me any longer,
small bird with the brown
flecked wings—
I have held out my hands
on this mountain
for so long
that my desire lines
are planted deep across
the rise of my palms.

—*L.L. Barkat*

5

Open Your Throat

Poetry in Song

Mom sang all the time, while passing from room to room, and especially when she was cooking. Sometimes she had music playing in the background, sometimes not. She sang Christmas songs at non-Christmasy times. I don't remember many details, just the singing.

Cancer treatment brings with it odd side effects, including, for my mother, difficulty breathing. Her doctor put her on the same medication I take for asthma. I saw the purple disk lying on her bathroom counter and told her I had the same prescription. She offered it to me since she wasn't using it.

"I couldn't sing when I was taking it," she explained.

My mother wasn't in a choir. She didn't sing solos. But she loved to sing, and she wasn't about to take something that would keep her from a daily source of delight.

That asthma medicine has taken my voice from a bold first soprano to a twerky tenor, so I'm embarrassed to even sing in the car. But when I cook, I turn on music—maybe George Strait, maybe Patty Griffin—and hum along while swinging my hips from the sink to the stove. It's a small kitchen. I don't have far to swing.

When I read this poem, I thought of my mother, opening her throat and releasing her song into the air. Her singing must have influenced me because I sang in choirs from sixth grade through my freshman year in college.

What to sing

My heart quieted,
and after being still awhile
a single word rose from
the heart of my listening
telling me, quite clearly,

> *Consider me,*
> *what I might mean, and*
> *how you might*
> *sing me.*

(I am not telling you the word,
it is private.)

Hoping so deeply
for my word to be true,
I sat, waiting to
discern. And there,
balanced on
a swaying branch
above my head
was a woman bird,
singing exactly what
my heart had heard.

She sang, *It's simple.*

Just open your throat.
The air will carry it.

—*Luci Shaw*

One of my jobs in high school was to organize the choir closet —boxes and boxes of songs in four-part or eight-part harmony. Our library included three categories of choral music: sacred, secular, and Christmas. Sacred music was hymns. The Broadway show tunes were in the secular section. The Christmas music included a little bit of everything. It had Handel's "Messiah" and "Santa Claus Is Comin' to Town" and "Amahl and the Night Visitors" and "Let It Snow."

Poetry is like that Christmas section. It's a hodgepodge— some fun, some serious, some rhyming, some in iambic pentameter, some with excessive dashes, some that tell a story, some that is nothing less than a song.

When people tell me they don't like poetry, I want to ask if they don't like songs either. If they're purists, they would only have classical music or yoga ditties loaded on their listening devices. Even poetry haters have songs that speak to them solely because of the words. On sunny days most folks are not going to roll down their car windows and belt out a poem—perhaps they should—but they will turn up the volume to their favorite tune and sing along. More than likely, the words rhyme.

There are folks who, if they admit to liking poetry, prefer that it rhyme. Maybe because that's the only type of poetry they've ever read, or maybe because when it rhymes, it seems more like a song.

When my son saw some of my poetry, he pointed out that it didn't rhyme, but hip-hop does. Agreed. Hip-hop contains rhymes I didn't know were possible.

Rosanne Cash, whose music is a little more my style than hip-hop, said there is a difference between her songs that are just songs and her songs that are poetry. In an interview on the podcast *On Being*, Cash talked about the song "God Is in the Roses," which she wrote the day after the death of her father, Johnny Cash. The song has deep personal meaning, but she wasn't sure it would stand alone as poetry without the aid of the music.

There are songs I wouldn't like without the backbeat, and there are others that touched me first because of the words. I often look up song lyrics on the Internet. Once upon a time I had to purchase the entire album/cassette/CD to get that information. Are the lyrics worth anything apart from the music? The songwriters think so. After some fighting back and forth between lyrics websites and music publishers, more sites are paying songwriters for the value of their words alone.

When a song has been around for a long time, like a hymn, it's almost impossible to separate the tune from the words. I first heard "Uncloudy Day" as performed by Willie Nelson on his album *The Troublemaker*. Mom loved that entire album and especially that song. The original hymn was titled "The Unclouded Day," and it dates back to around 1879.

When we went to see the place my mother picked to be buried, a cremation garden surrounded by the natural landscaping prized in the Texas Hill Country, on a cliff above a lake, something happened to remind me of that hymn.

Uncloudy Day

Cloudless days are bad days,
my son says
(hence, half a lifetime of bad

days for this Texas boy).
He comes with us this afternoon with full sun
to see the spot where Mom will be buried. But

when we arrive, look down at the plot,
he touches my arm, points up
at the one lone cloud in the sky.

Mom had her picture taken with her five grandkids for a book with profiles of cancer survivors and their grandchildren titled *The Smile Never Fades*. Their photo made the cover.

That was my mother's style—a professional photograph rather than a poem. If she had been the type of person to write poetry, I feel sure it would have rhymed. She might have even hummed a tune to go along with it.

There is a type of poem that means "little song," a sonnet. Sonnets are often love poems, but instead of romantic love, this one is about the love of a daughter for her mother. There are a couple of different types of sonnets, and each one has different rhyming rules, none of which mattered to me when I read this poem. I didn't even realize it was a sonnet until I read it aloud and heard the rhymes.

With My Mother,
Missing the Train

She was always late. At the final minute
we'd run for the city train, which roared right past,
its line of faces scanning us not in it.
The world was turned to terror by the blast
of hot departing wheels. Air seized my mother,
crushing her flustered skirts into a flurry
with me there clinging. Hush, there'll be another,
she'd say to keep me calm. No need to worry.
But there was a need. The speed of things was true
and rushing traffic urged us both ahead.
I wanted to race again, to burst right through
and make the great train wait. She never said
that missing things was serious, till I grew.
She held my hand more tightly than I knew.

—*Helena Nelson*

There are two reasons I didn't notice this poem's rhymes.
The first is a fancy term called *enjambment*, which means a sen-
tence doesn't end at the end of the line—it carries over, as many
of the sentences in this poem do. Enjambment hides rhymes so
the poem doesn't sound like a greeting card.

A second reason I didn't notice the rhymes is that they pair
single words with phrases, or they mismatch the number of syl-
lables. *Minute* rhymes with *in it. Mother* with *another. Ahead* and

said. Those rhymes are more interesting than the perfect rhymes like *flurry* and *worry*, though *flurry* is a terrific word.

Worry. There's a lot of it in this poem. Instead of telling us, "My mother was afraid," the poet shows us, "Air seized my mother,/crushing her flustered skirts into a flurry." The only thing happening in that sentence is that the wind ruffled the mother's skirt. But no, the air "seized" her, "crushing" her skirts, those "flustered" skirts.

The daughter is afraid, too. Her fear is focused on the train speeding away. She knows there is a need for "speed," for "rushing." She "wanted to race" and "to burst right through" despite the fact that her mother told her, "No need to worry."

Where are they going? What might it mean that they didn't make this train? Will there be another? I get the feeling that this missed train is one more missed opportunity in a lifetime of missed opportunities for this mother.

The last two lines are more traditional rhymes. That's a sonnet thing. The end is supposed to pack a punch and be almost its own couplet, or two-line rhyme. The end is the heart of the poem because it explains something about this mother-daughter relationship. Look who is clinging—the mother: "She held my hand more tightly than I knew."

Mom was not a clinger. But I have clung to my children, especially since losing my mother. I've done it twice while traveling, when we experienced weather delays. If my children were to write a sonnet, or even a three-line haiku, about traveling with me, it would be set in an airport. The mother would be early but an absolute wreck. She would be clinging too tightly. The child would step into the adult role, like the time my son used his own money to buy me a nap pillow at the Salt Lake City airport, or the time my daughter helped me navigate out of the maze that is Denver International.

But maybe my mother did cling to me without my knowing it, like when she and I went to New England together when I was 15. She and Dad were supposed to take a romantic vacation, but he couldn't go, so she invited me to come along. Not having my dad there forced my mother out of her comfort zone to do all the driving and deciding from town to town, state to state. She clung to me as her navigator, which was a tragic mistake, as I have no sense of direction. One day we were heading for Freeport, Maine, and we discovered we had taken a wrong turn only when we saw a sign proclaiming, "Welcome to New Hampshire!"

We laughed about our misadventure that night at dinner, when she ordered wild blueberry pie. She invited me to share, but I kept my fork to myself.

Why? Because I had an eating disorder and didn't realize it. Mom did, though.

During that trip she confronted me about my anorexia. When we got home, she arranged for me to get counseling. And when that didn't cut it, she found a place for me to get treatment. She didn't just fight her own battles with cancer; she helped me fight my battles, too. Even if I didn't want that help.

A couple of years later, when John and I were dating, he came with our family on vacation to South Padre. One night after dinner he and I took a run on the beach. When we came back, Mom was mad.

"I'd rather see you making out with John than running with him," she said. I was only two years out of treatment. I was not healed. She was right to be worried.

On the other hand, she was a woman who saw absolutely no good that could come from a run along the beach at sunset—not for anyone—whereas making out might very well lead to happily ever after.

6

Brilliantly Hydrated

Love Poetry

It was strange in my mother's last years to see pictures of her in the mountains, fly rod in hand. Growing up, we were beach people. Of course, South Padre Island is a day trip, and Colorado is a two-day trip. It took a long time for me to realize why she loved both the beach and the mountains: because of Chile.

My parents met in Chile as exchange students from the University of Texas in 1965. Chile is a long, skinny country in South America, with mountains lining one side and beaches lining the other. My parents fell in love there and had their first kiss at Quintero on *la playa de los enamorados*, "the beach of the lovers."

Mom was already fluent in Spanish after spending a summer in Mexico City after high school, so she did a lot of translating. My dad they called Cowboy, although he grew up on a farm — no cows, no horses. Since my parents met in a Spanish-speaking country, Spanish was their love language.

One day my husband, John, was visiting with a man who knew my mother back in college. He asked him what he remembered about Merry Nell.

"Oh, she was so wonderful," the man said, and then he paused and added, "What a loss."

On the trip Dad met Pablo Neruda, Chile's most famous poet. My dad was part of an informal get-together at the home of another poet, Nicanor Parra, and Neruda was there. At the time, he was too young to appreciate the significance of the visit, since poetry was not a part of this farm boy's life. He did not read Neruda until after my mother died. When he did, he was enchanted.

"I've wasted a lot of time not reading Neruda," he said.

I had not spent any significant time with Neruda either, although in a daily diet of poetry, I couldn't help but come across some of his poems. I'd even printed a couple to save in poetry scrapbooks. But I had my Neruda encounter on a trip to Bonners Ferry, Idaho.

It was Memorial Day weekend and John and I were on a trip. After we checked into our hotel, I walked downtown in search of an independent bookstore and found one—Bonners Books. Its tagline is "27 years of improbability," and how improbable was it that I found a book of Neruda's poetry called *Cien sonetos de amor*, or *100 Love Sonnets*, published by the University of Texas Press? Improbable? Yes. Impossible? No. Pure poetry? Absolutely.

I rushed back to our hotel room overlooking the Kootenai River and began to read. The edition had the original poems in Spanish on the left pages and the English translations on the right.

The poems were sensual and unusual. "Sonnet 16" used astronomy images—planet, star, universe, constellations, meteor, moon, sun, globe—in ways NASA never considered. I read "Sonnet 33" and then "Sonnet 100." (Who says you have to read poems in the order they're written?) I thought a lot about my parents, who taught me over their 43-year marriage to never take a loved one for granted.

On our trip, I realized I had been taking John for granted. Work had been busy, family had been busy, and although we went on the occasional lunch date, all we ever talked about was What Was Wrong. Then I discovered love poetry. First, Neruda. Later, others.

I'd been stuck in poems about death and flowers when I started reading L.L. Barkat's collection *Love, Etc.* I brought it with me into a hot bath, extra bubbly. I lit a candle and turned my Internet radio to piano solos. A song came up from some album called *Deep Joy.* My joy that night was shallower than the water in the tub.

Then I started reading the section called "Sexy Pie." I particularly liked "Sara Teasdale," which describes how she burned her dirty limericks. Maybe there were people she didn't want to read them, people she didn't want to know her mind wandered down those paths, as everyone's mind does. The poem ends, "and, my God, don't we need/somebody to love the side of us/we are always burning for fear?"

John knocked on the door. "Can I get you anything? I'm going to the store."

"Topo Chico," I told him. "Get the biggest bottle they have."

Topo Chico® is a bottled, sparkling mineral water from Mexico that claims to have healing powers because, legend has it, the spring water once cured an ailing Aztec princess. John didn't know what Topo Chico was, since his drown-your-sorrows beverage is Dr Pepper®, so I described the label, which features a princess cupping her hands to drink from the stream.

John came home with three bottles of Topo Chico. I drank them all while he made dinner. Then I opened my inbox and read this poem.

Bottled Water

I go to the corner liquor store
for a bottle of water, middle
of a hectic day, must get out
of the office, stop making decisions,
quit obsessing does my blue skirt clash
with my hot pink flats; should I get
my mother a caregiver or just put her
in a home, and I pull open the glass
refrigerator door, am confronted
by brands—Arrowhead, Glitter Geyser,
Deer Park, spring, summer, winter water,
and clearly the bosses of bottled water:
Real Water and Smart Water—how different
will they taste? If I drink Smart Water
will I raise my IQ but be less authentic?
If I choose Real Water will I no longer
deny the truth, but will I attract confused,
needy people who'll take advantage
of my realness by dumping their problems
on me, and will I be too stupid to help them
sort through their murky dilemmas?
I take no chances, buy them both,
sparkling smart, purified real, drain both bottles,
look around to see is anyone watching?
I'm now brilliantly hydrated.

—*Kim Dower*

I love a poem that is both funny and poignant.

The speaker has a dilemma. It's hidden in these lines, "should I get/my mother a caregiver or just put her/in a home." But before referring to the real problem, she mentions a trivial one: "does my blue skirt clash/with my hot pink flats." It's a question, but it doesn't have a question mark. I get the feeling this woman has spent the whole morning bothered about her clothes clashing instead of obsessing about the real problem, her mother's care.

This is a woman for whom this decision should be easy, at least in the context of her work. All day at the office she makes decisions, but she can't seem to make this one. Why not? Well, this one's a biggie. It requires leaving the office—"middle/of a hectic day/must get out." And notice where she buys the water, at "the corner liquor store." I didn't even know liquor stores sold bottled water. Perhaps she considered buying something with a harder edge, then changed her mind.

Choosing which bottled water to buy can be daunting on the best of days. Each brand sounds clean and clear and health-full, "spring, summer, winter water." I don't think I'd buy Autumn Water. I'd be afraid of having to fish out fallen leaves first. The speaker narrows her selection to the "bosses," Real Water and Smart Water. She stands in front of the refrigerator, door open, deciding.

When I read this part of the poem I thought of a friend who lost her son-in-law to suicide. The next morning she sat down at the kitchen to make a grocery list. She couldn't decide whether to use a pen or a pencil, so she didn't make the list. She never made it to the grocery store. That's how this moment feels to me. Real or Smart? Pen or pencil? Caregiver or nursing home?

Finally the poet takes no chances and buys both bottles, "sparkling smart, purified real." Then she wastes no time. She doesn't just drink both bottles, she "drains" them, as I drained those three bottles of Topo Chico.

Four months after our trip to Idaho, John and I took another trip to South Padre Island. We're learning the importance of doing what my parents always did—getting away together. Being at the Texas Gulf Coast, a mile or so down the beach from where we stayed when I was a kid, made me feel close to my mother. In the afternoons John and I sat under a pop-up gazebo and watched the waves. In the evenings we sat on the patio and looked at the night sky. When we came home, we felt like a new couple. No wonder my parents took so many trips. Perhaps they made time for trips because they met on one. They were never stingy with I-love-you's.

But I was. With John, and also my mother. Even though I grew up knowing she would probably die from the disease, I was a hateful teenage daughter. I mellowed after marriage and kids, but I wasn't exactly warm. I tried to make up for it during her last three years by going to those chemotherapy appointments, spending a week with her instead of skiing, taking that trip to Creede.

As 2010 dawned, Mom realized each treatment was buying her a shorter amount of time—no longer months and not even weeks. Possibly only days. Was it worth it? In February she decided it wasn't. It was time to call hospice.

Valentine's Chai

Sitting in a sunny cafe, I call my parents
because I can't stand to hear
bad news at home.
So I call from here, on my cell,
armed with chai.

She's telling the doctor, *No more.*

She will leave his office with some pills
that will lengthen her sweet tooth in time
for Valentine's Day.

I quaff my tea and head to the store
for candy hearts, chocolate hearts,
Reese's peanut butter hearts, heart-shaped
cookies piled with icing—any
confectionary way to say *I love you I love
you I love you I love you I love you.*

7

Get Out the Eggs

Weird Poets

Mom always had a sweet tooth, and it seemed to get sweeter as she declined. During her last few months she abandoned healthy eating. She ate what she could keep down, and more often than not, that was sugar. She ate apple pie when she should have been eating Thanksgiving dinner, chocolate chip cookies when she should have been eating barbecue, flan after she pushed around the Mexican food on her plate to make it look like she'd eaten it. Her last meal was cherry pie.

One of my favorite memories of her is from our vacation in Creede, when she joyfully got out the marshmallows and chocolate bars and graham crackers so we could roast s'mores.

My poem "S'More" was published in *The Cancer Poetry Project 2: more poems by cancer patients and those who love them*, edited by Karin B. Miller. After my copy came in, I spent a Sunday morning watching YouTube videos, which several of the contributors posted of themselves reading their poems. I couldn't resist looking at the number of views—37, 40, 114. In the column beside the videos, where YouTube uses its magical algorithms to decide what else I might like to see, there was a video titled *How I Survived Cancer with Alternative* ... I couldn't bear to read the rest of the title, although I'm sure it promised a miracle cure. That video had 25,887 views.

Poetry isn't generally popular. It doesn't often get a bunch of likes and favorites and thumbs up. It usually impacts people in the tens, not the ten thousands. Sometimes we write for an audience of one, just to help us remember.

S'More

On a cool summer evening in the San Juans
we gather around a chimenea to make s'mores.
Chocolate and graham crackers are no match
for our family's flaming marshmallows.
The kids shout how best to roast puffed sugar.
We smush sticky fingers into the bag
grab our prey
perfect our technique
poke sticks into the fire over and over again.

"We should sing Kumbaya," Mom says.

We laugh though
it doesn't seem like a time for camp songs.
We need sweet summer blues
during this, our last vacation together.

Mom extends her stick into the flames,
her short, marshmallow hair bleached white
by chemo. The fire of her cancer contained
for now
in a vessel we can still jab with prayers.

We devour each bright moment
as if her bag of marshmallows will never run out.

Mom didn't tell us in Colorado that her right eye was beginning to see in sepia tones. When she returned to Texas, an ocular oncologist discovered the cancer had spread to her right retinal artery and brain. But I knew none of that while roasting s'mores, with a cup of hot tea in hand.

I drink tea because of my mother. She had a tea drawer; I have a tea cabinet. Nothing makes me happier than when a friend sends a single teabag in the mail. If Mom were to see my blog, how the entire theme is red teacups, I think she'd take credit.

Since her death, Dad gives me things of hers. Each item is specific—not, *Take all her clothes*, but, *Take this jacket. Take these sunglasses. Take this teapot.*

The teapot he bequeathed to me is a Chatsford and has colorful flowers. I would never have purchased it for myself. I like things flowerless. But because it is my mother's, I've used it every day for the last five years. Until I broke the lid.

I was on the back porch, sitting at the octagonal picnic table I use as a writing desk. I don't even know how I dropped the lid, but it shattered on the concrete. I sobbed as if my mother had died anew.

Then I went inside and baked muffins.

I can always bake. I started baking when I was 10 years old, when my mother first got cancer. When necessary, I made my own birthday cakes, always lemon. In middle school I baked mini-loaves for friends as Christmas gifts. Baking is something I can always do, something almost immediately gratifying.

When I find a poem about baking, I save it. It seems that

poets—usually women poets—understand baking as a sacred act. It has magical powers. It can beat back depression because it proclaims either to the baker or to the eater, "You're not worthless! These muffins are fabulous!"

On the Eve of Your Thirteenth Birthday
for Jeffrey

the last day of twelve
was nothing special,
you said.
you didn't dress for gym,
didn't play four-square with
the others. only walked,
you said.

In English, you wrote
a myth...about Gusano—
it means *worm* in Spanish
you said.
this Greco-Spanish
worm-god found freedom,
you said.
but he led his people
back into the
earth to rule the Underworld
and that's why he will
be responsible for
the zombie apocalypse,
you said.

and math was about
interest, like money and
banks, you know?
you said.
and you have homework
so you came home in
a bad mood and didn't
want to talk about twelve
you said.

so i hushed and got out
the eggs, cracked them one-by-
one in the bowl and mixed until
those yellow eyes are gone; i
rubbed grease on the pan that is
swathed in black enamel
from years of cradling sweet
batter...and i poured more
in. you at the table building
up interest when the room
starts to smell like a birthday.

and suddenly, you are there,
beside to lick the batter from
the bowl. what time was I
born?
you said.

—*Laura Boggess*

What baker has not imagined eyes in the eggs? I also love "when the room/starts to smell like a birthday." Isn't that better than if she'd said, "the cake smelled like it was done"? Soon that boy will turn 16 and spend his birthday with his girlfriend. He won't want his mom to bake. Maybe she'll feel sad and go into the kitchen and bake anyway. Or write another poem.

Grace Paley wrote a poem called "The Poet's Occasional Alternative," in which the speaker bakes a pie instead of writing a poem because she knows the pie will be good—the poem? Hard to tell.

Some days I know better than to write my way out of pain. So the day I broke the teapot lid and decided to bake banana chocolate chip muffins instead of trying to write a poem, it was the right decision. I gave thanks for bananas and for Nestlé's miniature chocolate chips. If Mom were sitting with me, sharing warm muffins and hot tea, reading a perfectly understandable baking poem, she might set it down, raise her eyebrows, and say, "But Megan, poets can be a little weird, right?"

Yes, Merry Nell, poets can be a little weird.

A lot of writers don't read poetry. A lot of readers don't read it either. Maybe because, let's face it, there's a problem with poets.

Sometimes poets are exactly like their stereotype. The men never wash their hair and they wear tweed, even in the summer. The women wear only black and have frizzy hair and look like they'd be more comfortable on a broomstick than in a pickup truck. They can't even operate the remote control. (Oops, that's me.) The good ones are alcoholics, and the great ones die too soon. They have a string of sad love affairs or even worse, no love at all, just a cat who ignores them. And they talk weird, too. They speak of inspiration and the Muse. They don't know where their poems come from or what they mean and shame on you for looking at them with a face that says you don't get them, for even thinking there is something to get in the first place.

Not all poets are the stereotype, certainly not those who bake. Many poets have real jobs. I know a poet who is a biochemist, one who's in the corporate world, one who runs a winery. William Carlos Williams was a doctor. Ted Kooser stayed in insurance for decades. The list goes on.

Add to that list Sally Clark. She is a poet, and she is unassuming. For much of her career she was a restaurateur. When she wants to relax, she balances her checkbook, which, admittedly, is odd, but not in way people think of poets as odd.

After working in an office in Dallas, she and her husband moved to the Texas Hill Country. They owned and operated a restaurant in the tourist town of Fredericksburg for 20 years. After they retired, Sally attended a writers retreat and decided to try her hand at poetry. She was 47, young enough for a new career. Up until then she had never written anything other than a grocery list. With one exception—a journal she kept for her oldest granddaughter.

"When she was born, I started writing a journal to her, and when I went back and read it, I was bored." Sally thought, "This doesn't at all convey the emotion that I want it to. I could learn to do this better."

One of her friends started subscribing to *Writer's Digest* and saw an article about a poet she thought Sally might like. The poet was Ted Kooser.

"When I read his poetry, then I really got excited. I understood his poems. They were so clear. It was so good to know that's a viable way to write," Sally said. "He says he writes three or four poems every day, and at the end of the month he has three or four poems that are publishable. He gives himself permission to write crummy poetry."

When she finds a poem she likes, Sally will Google the author and read more of the poet's work. If she finds several things she likes, then she'll buy a collection or check it out at the library.

"I completely understand why people don't like poetry and don't write poetry and don't read poetry because so much of it is incomprehensible. I like to read the U. S. poet laureates, and all of it is clear, understandable. It means something," she notes. "You can't read everything, so you might as well read the best."

Sally admits some of her poetry is crummy. She keeps writing. In 2013, she made 127 submissions. That was a down year. "I usually do 300 some-odd."

Of those 127 submissions, 18 were accepted, 92 were rejected, and she's still waiting to hear back on 17. Sometimes the same poem will fare differently in different contests. One particular poem has won two first place awards, one second place, one third place, and one honorable mention. It has lost in 19 other contests.

Sally is also the most practical poet I know. Inspiration, *schmin*spiration. She writes for money. Not a lot of money, of course, but enough to support her habit. She began by entering a poetry contest rather than submitting to a publisher because she didn't have to write a cover letter—an intimidating task for a new poet.

"I didn't have anything to say in a cover letter, so I thought, 'I'll enter this contest.' I put the envelope in the mail and thought to myself, 'You would rather spend $3 than send a cover letter.'" She recalls, "I won 2nd place! And I was hooked."

For a year Sally wrote more than 20 units of poetry for a homeschool publisher, and each unit contained 30 specific types of poems on a variety of subjects, from pumpkins to castles. Give her a topic or a prompt or a theme, and she'll write. In order to learn about a subject, her first stop is the children's section of the library.

"Like when I wrote about castles, I found easy readers that had beautiful drawings of castles. I thought, 'I can stare at this picture and imagine if I were walking in that building.' I just needed visual images."

With most of her extended family living in town, Sally doesn't have time to write an epic novel. Poetry is the right size for her.

"If you're writing a novel, you have to set aside chunks of time to write. But poetry can slip in and out of your day. It fits into my life without interrupting my life," she notes. "There's nothing like reading your genre. If you write novels, you've got to read novels. That takes a lot of time. Poetry, it can be done first thing in the morning, in the bathroom."

In 2015, Sally published a pop-up board book titled *Where's My Hug?*. After the publisher accepted the manuscript, the editor emailed her a contract and attached some revisions.

"Who knew 35 words would need revisions?" Sally joked. Only a poet, and so she revised.

8

Ten Thousand Daffodils

Understanding Poetry

Mom's dining room table always had a vase of fresh flowers, whether they were yellow roses from my dad or a seasonal bouquet she picked up at the grocery store. As I write this morning, I am looking at a vase of yellow tulips my husband bought for me. Same color, different bloom.

Sometimes my mother saw flowers as a sign. While I was writing my 72 cancer poems, she was writing 29 emails to friends and supporters—full of faith, hope, and love. In the one dated July 9, 2009, she wrote,

> On Tuesday and Wednesday, May 26th & 27th, I was feeling anxious. I went outside Tuesday morning, up my front walk, and discovered a green plant, about 3-4 inches in width, growing *through* the cement that bonds the stones together. I noted there was a lovely purple flower blooming on the plant. I took this as a sign and as a promise that the things I was worried about would get better. I felt cheered and uplifted. On the following morning, Wednesday May 27th, I went to see if the same plant

was still there. And there it was, thrusting up between the stones, with a new purple flower gracing it. This event might not have seemed miraculous if this plant had not totally disappeared by that same Wednesday afternoon when I went to get the mail. No plant, no leaves, no flowers, no nothing where it had been poking through the stony surface of my stone walkway just that morning.

The day I re-read Mom's letter, I spied a purple flower growing in our alley amid weeds and unmown grass. Between the trash can and the gas meter stood spring. At first I thought her choice of the word *miraculous* was a little strong. Maybe I was mistaken.

Like any good Texas gal, Mom loved bluebonnets, the state flower. Lady Bird Johnson, former first lady, made sure they were sown alongside highways across the state. They crop up in the heart of Texas in early spring. People often take Easter photos in a field of blue. But bluebonnets don't last long—less than a month, usually. As the weather warms into the 90s, they fade, making way for the warmer wildflowers, the reds and yellows.

Every morning I walk my dogs, and about a block away from my house stands a patch of bluebonnets in another alley. They are usually the first and the last blooms of the season. In 2009, that clump of bluebonnets would not die. They came in April, stayed through May and into June. They were still there in July. How is that even botanically possible? And how was my mother managing so well after another wretched season of chemo?

Still

A clump of bluebonnets stands in the alley
long past
Memorial Day. Usually they're fried by Easter.

In the spring they grow
in green pastures,
beside busy highways.

Now they look tired, out of place,
like they didn't get the notice that it's time
to make room for the warm wildflowers.

Tomorrow is Independence Day, and they're still there
barely blue.
The Mexican hats, the wine cups, even

the firewheels have faded.
Those stubborn bluebonnets hang on
like my mother

still thriving through cancer
after cancer
after cancer.

By the time the following spring blossomed, she was gone.
The year she died Central Texas had the best wildflowers any-

one could remember since the drought started—not only blue-bonnets but also Indian paintbrush, white poppies, purple salvia, beautiful yellow bitterweed.

"Joy is, in a way, sorrow's flower," writes Christian Wiman in *My Bright Abyss*. Wiman, former editor of *Poetry* magazine, has a rare form of cancer. His memoir is about poetry and faith and love and death.

Love and death are two of the great poetic themes. Faith is in there, too. There are a surprising number of poems about poetry (write what you know). The rest are about flowers.

Poetry has been criticized for featuring too many flowers, and who has time for such sentimentality? Forget poetry. It's froufrou.

Perhaps the most famous flower poem is by William Wordsworth, the fellow with a fetish for daffodils.

I Wandered Lonely as a Cloud

I wandered lonely as a cloud
   That floats on high o'er vales and hills,
When all at once I saw a crowd,
   A host, of golden daffodils;
Beside the lake, beneath the trees,
Fluttering and dancing in the breeze.

Continuous as the stars that shine
   And twinkle on the Milky Way,
They stretched in never-ending line
   Along the margin of a bay:

Ten thousand saw I at a glance,
Tossing their heads in sprightly dance.

The waves beside them danced, but they
   Out-did the sparkling waves in glee:
A Poet could not but be gay,
   In such a jocund company:
I gazed—and gazed—but little thought
What wealth the show to me had brought:

For oft, when on my couch I lie
   In vacant or in pensive mood,
They flash upon that inward eye
   Which is the bliss of solitude;
And then my heart with pleasure fills,
And dances with the daffodils.

    —William Wordsworth

Do you think Wordsworth literally danced? Maybe he got off his couch, grabbed a golden flower from a vase and pranced around the room—you never can tell with poets. Why is he in love with daffodils? Is it a metaphor? Did he miss his calling to be a florist? Or maybe the poem is about being captivated by beauty and later trying to recapture the memory and emotion.

No one understands a poet like another poet. Thank you, Joyce Sutphen, for helping me understand Wordsworth's poem with your own:

The Wordsworth Effect

Is when you return to a place
and it's not nearly as amazing
as you once thought it was,

or when you remember how you felt
about something (or someone) but you know
you'll never feel that way again.

It's when you notice someone has turned
down the volume, and you realize
it was you; when you have the

suspicion that you've met the enemy
and you are it, or when you get
your best ideas from your sister's journal.

Is also—to be fair—the thing that enables
you to walk for miles and miles chanting to
yourself in iambic pentameter

and to travel through Europe with
only a clean shirt, a change of
underwear, a notebook and a pen.

And yes: is when you stretch out
on your couch and summon up ten thousand
daffodils, all dancing in the breeze.

—*Joyce Sutphen*

The one time I went to England, back in college, I brought multiple clean shirts. I had a notebook and a pen and never used them to write poetry. However, if I lie still, I can remember that summer. I can remember how Diet Coke® tasted different when I had to walk a mile from Westminster School to buy one. I remember feeling scared when I got lost in a maze at Hampton Court Palace. I can hear the guy, chained to a pole, wearing only underwear, shouting profanity in Leicester Square. And none of this comes back to me in iambic pentameter.

Reading Sutphen's poem about Wordsworth made me re-read Wordsworth, and then go back to Sutphen. I am the one who turns the music down. When I sit to write, it feels like everything good has already been written. With each passing year I appreciate bluebonnets more, yet somehow they're always better in my memory, and my memory always skips over the fact that the best bluebonnets are always found in alleys.

Without the assistance of a poet like Joyce Sutphen, Wordsworth loses me. But taking poems in small doses, one a day or even one a week, is like a soaker hose for the soul.

Another poetry service I recommend, besides *Every Day Poems* from *Tweetspeak*, is *American Life in Poetry*, curated by Ted Kooser, U. S. poet laureate from 2004-2006. But don't do it just for the poems—do it for the introductions, which Kooser calls *columns*.

These are the shortest columns I've ever read, usually two or three sentences long. Poetic terminology? None. Kooser generally takes one sentence to explain why he liked the poem and then another to explain something about the poet. He always mentions what state the poet is from. His columns never delve into meaning, leaving that up to the reader.

Often after reading the poem, I re-read the introduction and marvel. Only a poet could use such precise language to introduce poetry, and only Kooser can do it in such a casual, nonthreatening way, as if you had an uncle who, after serving you a breakfast of coffee and biscuits, were to say, "By the way, got a poem you might like."

One day I emailed Sally Clark to make sure she had read that day's edition of *American Life in Poetry*, "Love Poem," by Melissa Balmain. However, I didn't read it until a day after the email arrived. Sally thought I meant a different poem of the day, one by William Wordsworth, the daffodil dude.

She wrote, "Hmmm.....I got lost in it. :(too sophisticated for me?" This is a perfectly acceptable response to any poem, but especially a poem from a different century.

The poem I'd recommended wasn't sophisticated. It rhymed. It was almost a song. It reminded me of a marriage poem Sally had written. I told her I was surprised she didn't like it and then we figured out the mixup. She not only understood the poem but "absolutely loved it."

"How are you doing?" I wrote back. "I was worried when you said you didn't get the poem. Since you thought it was the Wordsworth one, I'm not so worried. But I thought I'd ask."

Sally's husband has cancer. Until he was diagnosed a couple of years ago, she hadn't known anyone with the disease other than her hairdresser. It's been a rough awakening. If she didn't fall in love with a sweet, rhyming poem about marriage, then something must be wrong.

She stopped writing poetry after her husband's diagnosis

because she did not want to write about cancer. Living with it every day was hard enough—she didn't want to write about it, too. She tried to write about other things, but eventually those springs dried up. It was as if an enormous fountain was gushing right in the middle of her living room, and she kept walking around it saying, "Nope. Nope. Nope."

Finally, Sally realized she could write poems about cancer … secretly. No one ever had to see them.

"I chose a green notebook to write them in because green is my least favorite color."

Out of writing those difficult poems in the ugly notebook, she wrote one about dust. "My lord, the dust in my house," she told me. "But it's good. That's one I'll try to publish at some point."

That's what happens. In the middle of writing bad cancer poetry, she wrote a good one about something everyone can relate to.

Why is there so much dust in Sally's house? Because she's not cleaning. Why isn't she cleaning? Because of her husband's cancer. Her life revolves around taking care of him, attending events for her five grandchildren, or participating in one of the three, sometimes four, writing groups she attends. Dust is a symbol of all that's left undone.

Sometimes the good poem is hidden, like a single penny at the bottom of a fountain. The more you write, the more the flow stops coming out of the center of the kitchen and from the keyboard or the lucky pencil. Then a non-cancerous poem sneaks into the ugly green notebook.

Unattended

I love to write at dusk,
that time of the day
when the shift is changing,
the sun is clocking out
and the moon is running late
and for just a little while
the sky
is left unattended.

—*Sally Clark*

Dusk was Mom's favorite time of day.

9

A Radish Rises

Weird Poetry

My favorite tea roadie is a tall, clay-lined mug that changes color depending on the temperature of the liquid inside. When the cup is cold, the cylinder looks mostly brown. When I add hot water, the scene changes to blue. At first I didn't even notice the orange, but it shows up in different spots depending on whether the background is blue or brown.

Poetry is like that roadie—its meaning shifts according to mood. Weird, but wonderful.

When people say they don't like poetry, they often mean they don't like the weird stuff. And let's face it, some of it is awfully strange. Not all good poetry is weird, and not all weird poetry is good. I tend to like straightforward poems, but every now and then I like a little mystery.

I attended a poetry workshop with Dr. Benjamin Myers, poet and professor at Oklahoma Baptist University, and he brought three weird poems—his word—for us to read.

After the workshop I called Ben to ask for his thoughts on weird poetry.

"A lot of times people who aren't acclimated to poetry expect a poem to be accessible in the way an essay is accessible —with a clear message or point—when often a poem can seem very obscure and yet, clearly an emotion or a mood is being conveyed," he said.

Ben's word *acclimated* is key. Unless poetry is already your thing, don't start with the weird stuff. Get acclimated first.

He brought John Berryman's "Dream Song 14" to the workshop. It's not the kind of poem I usually like because it's a tad obscure. Actually, it's totally bizarre. Since then I've read it countless times, and I still don't know what it means. But each time I find something new to like. Ben said Berryman's poem is a good example of what makes a poem a poem: It says things in a way no other form of writing can.

"At the end of that poem—'leaving/behind: me, wag'—there's no paraphrasable way to state that. There's no translation into prose for that line, but it leaves you with a sense of [Berryman's] humorous side, his mirthful reflection."

Sometimes poets play with words, using them like a giant tub of blocks to see what they can build.

"A lot of poets are interested in finding out what poetry can do, playfully and experimentally exploring possibilities for alternative kinds of communication," Ben said.

I asked him what non-weird poets he likes.

"Jane Kenyon is one of my all-time favorites, very subtle and very direct." He continued, "William Stafford. He sort of straddles the line between the weird and the direct. 'Traveling Through the Dark' is a very accessible poem that says more than it says."

When our writers group read Stafford's poem, we launched into a discussion of Deer Encounters, since our corner of the state has more white-tailed deer than humans. But I've read the poem several times since. It's also about what we do when we encounter the unthinkable and how we face it in ourselves.

Ben also recommended the poetry of Frank O'Hara, who "wrote very readable, very accessible poems that were highly influenced by abstract expressionism and art in the '50s. He was also making poems out of common experiences, what he called 'I do this, I do that' poems, where he writes about what he does."

I was not familiar with O'Hara, but his poem "Mayakovsky" made it into an episode of the TV series *Mad Men*. Mr. O'Hara, you summed up the unsummupable Don Draper.

Ben's own poetry is not weird. It has a lot of depth, but the images and settings are concrete. I asked him where he thinks he falls on the weird scale.

"I do tend to aim more toward the accessible because I believe in poetry for a large audience. I'm in that camp with Dana Gioia, who blames modern poets for alienating the audience. If we want to get people to read poems, we've got to write poems they want to read."

Ben also mentioned Dylan Thomas, writer of "Do Not Go Gentle Into That Good Night," as a poet who could bridge the gap between obscurity and mystery. I asked Ben to explain the difference.

"When we encounter mystery in nature, our response is awe or wonder, unless you're a scientist and need to explain it. That should be the aim in a poem as well, to create a mystery that is nourishing or comforting rather than simply frustrating."

Then he said there is one kind of weird poetry we don't think of as weird—nursery rhymes. "When I think about the basic first poems we learn, the nursery rhymes, they carry so much mystery for us. A lot of them are coming out of now-meaningless context, the songs about London Bridge or the plague. The original meaning has been lost, but they still survive and carry a lot of power." Being involved with poetry, even nursery rhymes, he said, keeps us open to the power of language.

"My 9-year-old daughter is in love with reciting 'Jabberwocky,' which is complete nonsense, and that's one of the things she loves about it—the absurdity and the delight in language and sound," Ben shared.

Weird can be playful, like the Jabberwock. Or like Dr. Seuss, whose books are full of weirdness, yet generation after generation we read his rhyming stories to our little ones. Many times I've heard a person who doesn't care for poetry admit they like Shel Silverstein.

But Seuss and Silverstein are not the only poets who write for children. For more names, look up an article in *Poetry* magazine titled "All Good Slides Are Slippery," by Lemony Snicket, aka Daniel Handler, author of the 13-volume *A Series of Unfortunate Events*. In the article, Snicket offers a collection of poems he selected for children—what he called a "children's poetry portfolio." Snicket chose poems he liked. They aren't meant to teach kids something about poetry or convey a theme or educate in any way. He liked them, and he thought kids might like them, too:

> If you are a child, you might like these poems. Of course, you might not. Poems, like children, are individuals, and will not be liked by every single person who happens to come across them. So you may consider this portfolio a gathering of people in a room. It does not matter how old they are, or how old you are yourself. What matters is that there are a bunch of

people standing around in a room, and you
might want to look at them.

That's the best introduction to poetry I've ever read. Like people, sometimes you click with a poem. There are others you don't like much at first, but after you get to know them, you feel differently. Others never quite grow on you. The only unacceptable opinion is shunning.

This poem by children's poet Karla Kuskin is a nature poem about the moon. I've always had a thing for moon poems. In this poem—which is a little weird—she compares the moon to a radish, not by saying, "Shall I compare thee to a radish?" but by sticking a radish in the night sky, rising.

Write About a Radish

Write about a radish
too many people write about the moon.
The night is black
the stars are small and high
the clock unwinds its ever-ticking tune
hills gleam dimly
distant nighthawks cry.
A radish rises in the waiting sky.

—*Karla Kuskin*

Knowing this poem was written for children demystifies it for me. Look how Kuskin describes everything except the moon—

the night, the stars, the clock (that's my favorite part), the hills, the nighthawks. So much in only eight lines. The more I read it, the less weird I think it is.

I tried to write a moon poem once. Some of the lines echo the song "Blue Moon" written by Richard Rodgers and Lorenz Hart in 1934. I wrote it after my mother and I got into an argument about her treatment. It was hard to see her suffer, and she suffered so gracefully. I felt like a wretch for complaining when she never lost hope. Never.

Blue Moon

Mom gets two full moons, one early,
one on New Year's Eve eve when
we talk as only mothers and daughters can—
speech as rocky as the lunar surface.

After she's gone will I still orbit her earth?
Will her tides still move my every wave?

I am standing alone, waving goodbye.
She will ring in the new year with dreams in her heart,
with the love of her own dear husband, who adores her,
who wishes me a safe drive as I look
in my rearview mirror and the moon
has indeed turned to gold.

Her 23 unexpected years of remission were not blue moon months. They were blue moon years.

During her last three years I began to appreciate night. I've always been an early bird, a morning person, my father's daughter. Often I drove back from her appointments after the sun had gone down, and the next morning I'd be up early, walking the dogs before the sun rose. I live in a small town, small enough to see the moon and many stars. Those late drives and early walks made me appreciate the night sky in a way I never had. They made me look for loveliness.

Night

Stars over snow,
    And in the west a planet
Swinging below a star—
    Look for a lovely thing and you will find it,
It is not far—
    It will never be far.

—*Sara Teasdale*

10

Someone Came Knocking

Poetry in Fiction

After the argument with my mom, which resulted in my "Blue Moon" poem, I noticed a couple of lines from "Ode to a Nightingale" by John Keats. They appeared in a book of fiction, and there's nothing I love more than a well-placed poem within a story.

> Now more than ever seems it rich to die,
> To cease upon the midnight with no pain,

Thank you, Mr. Keats. That's what I was trying to say to my mother. When she did cease upon the midnight, it was with no pain.

If I had gone skiing with my family as planned, I could have avoided that argument (and, I suppose, the poem that sprang from it). But, on no more than a hunch, I decided to stay home with my mother. It was a tough week, cancer-wise. She was at the oncology center every day, first for chemotherapy, then to get treatments to counteract its side effects.

The Mimosa Lady

Tuesday, two ladies end chemo regimens
with the traditional confetti tossing and bell ringing.

Another woman throws a party
right there in the infusion room
mimosas for all.

"What's the occasion?" Mom asks.

"I've never had a break from chemo,"
The Mimosa Lady says, "and now I'm stage 4."

Mom announces, "I'm stage 4!"

"Then have a mimosa!"

Mom shakes her head.
"I can't. I'm still fighting."

The Mimosa Lady shakes her head right back.
"I'm dancing!"

When we weren't watching the Mimosa Lady or visiting with nurses or other patients, I was reading to my mother. The novella was Mark Salzman's *Lying Awake*. It's about a nun and a poet facing a health crisis that could cause her to lose her poetry, and possibly, her faith as well. It's my favorite book, filled with snippets of psalms and poems. Mom liked it, too, although we never finished it. After she died, I looked all over her bedroom for it, through all her stacks of books—on her bedside table, next to the chaise lounge, in her desk. I never found it. I don't know if she read the last chapter. She probably passed it on to a friend.

Mom enjoyed reading, but she rarely finished a book because she'd get distracted by the next book a friend recommended. In turn, she frequently recommended books she hadn't finished. But books were important to her. She often gave them as presents. The books she bought for my children were usually purchased at book signings, and she always told the author with great pride, "My daughter is a writer." As if I were in the same league with Madeleine L'Engle. Who she actually said that to.

In 1996, when I was six months pregnant, she and I went to a retreat to hear L'Engle speak. At the retreat Mom bought *A Wrinkle in Time* and had L'Engle autograph it for my baby.

L'Engle gave us an assignment to write a sonnet. She believed the structure of form poetry would free us to write better. She told us we could try either an Elizabethan (English) or a Petrarchan (Italian). I had no clue what she meant. But I knew immediately what I would write my sonnet about.

This was not my first pregnancy. Only nine months before, I'd lost a baby due to an ectopic pregnancy. The dates of the L'Engle retreat corresponded to my original due date. I was grateful to be pregnant again, but I wanted the first baby, too. Couldn't I have both? I never had the joy of telling everyone the big news because I found out I was pregnant in an ER and left the hospital a few days later, unpregnant. But if the first child had survived, this one wouldn't exist. Surely that was poetry material.

I finished the sonnet before breakfast on the last day. I wrote it in pencil, in a small spiral notebook, which is how and where I still write poems. The retreat center had swings everywhere, and one overlooked a cliff. It was right outside the room where my mother and I stayed. I loved to swing as a child, and I loved to jump off swings. When I'd swing on that one in the moonlight, it looked like I could jump off, over the river, past the canyon, straight to the moon. As I wrote the poem I imagined the first baby, a girl—I was sure of it—sitting next to me, swinging. We'd talk. I'd tell her about her soon-to-be baby brother.

After breakfast I took the poem to L'Engle, who said she liked it. Alas, I lost the sonnet. I don't know if it was actually good or if L'Engle just encouraged a young woman who needed it.

At the time, poetry had not been on my radar for several years. The act of writing a sonnet reminded me that I liked this sort of thing, although I didn't write any poems when my son was born three months later, or when my daughter was born three years after that. When my daughter went to preschool and my son went to kindergarten, I started reading a poem every day before I began to write, and poetry began to work on me again.

My first project was a middle-grade novel written from the perspective of a sixth-grade girl. It never jelled, but I still read middle grade and young adult fiction. I was thrilled when John Green wrote a bestseller about two teenagers with cancer who fall in love, called *The Fault in Our Stars*. Not only is it about cancer, it's filled with poetry.

I've read many interviews with Green and all the FAQs on his website, and so far no one has asked him about the poetry in his novels. It's just there. Which makes me so happy.

The narrator, Hazel Grace Lancaster, is an unusual young woman. She prefers to read poetry rather than write it, although she has plenty to write about—she's a 16-year-old with terminal cancer. But she thinks other poets have said it better, so she quotes from their work, including "There's a certain slant of light," by Emily Dickinson; "Degrees of Gray in Philipsburg," by Richard Hugo; "Sonnet 55," by William Shakespeare; "Howl," by Allen Ginsberg; "The Love Song of J. Alfred Prufrock," by T. S. Eliot; "Thirteen Ways of Looking at a Blackbird," by Wallace Stevens; and "Nothing Gold Can Stay," by Robert Frost.

Early in the novel, Hazel takes a twentieth-century American poetry class at a community college, and she says the professor talked about Sylvia Plath for an hour and a half without ever reading any of Plath's poetry. Plath deserves someone like Hazel, who will focus on her poetry rather than her biography.

In a column called "Poet's Choice" in *The Washington Post*, poet Linda Pastan wrote, "I often write poems in my head to distract myself during hard times. Some years ago after a car crash, while I lay waiting for the ambulance, I actually finished a poem I had been working on, determined not to die before I had it right." Guess who else writes a poem while waiting for an ambulance? Hazel. Hers is modeled on William Carlos Williams' "The Red Wheelbarrow," which she also recites in that scene. I've never understood "The Red Wheelbarrow," but I've always loved its images. Now when I read it, I think of Hazel. Re-reading Williams' poem, I see it differently. I have the context that narrative provides.

Green puts poems in his other novels, too. *Paper Towns* includes selections from Walt Whitman's "Song of Myself," which is used as part of a series of clues to find a character who has gone missing. In his first novel, *Looking for Alaska*, a couplet from "As I Walked Out One Evening" by W. H. Auden appears throughout the story: "You shall love your crooked neighbour/ With your crooked heart." I printed that poem years ago because of that very couplet, but having it as a thread in a novel helped me understand both the poem and the book more fully.

When reading John Green or another author who slips poetry into the story, stop and look up the poem, and then go back and re-read the section with the poem. After finishing the book, read the poem one more time to see if it was used as fore-shadowing or to provide insight into a character. A good writer doesn't stick a poem in a narrative without a reason.

If I could wave my magic wand, all poetry would be read aloud by the character Eleanor Douglas from Rainbow Rowell's young adult novel *Eleanor & Park*. After Mr. Stessman hears Eleanor read Emily Dickinson's "I had been hungry all the years" to his English class, he makes her his go-to reader. He can't wait for the class to get to their unit on Medea so Eleanor can read. When Eleanor is absent, Mr. Stessman says there's no point in reading *Macbeth* aloud without her. Only a handful of scenes from *Eleanor & Park* are set in the classroom, but those scenes and the poems referenced in them say something about Eleanor. The effect of her voice reveals something about her character we don't learn until later in the novel.

Originally, poetry was a spoken art form. When did that stop? When did we only read poetry and not listen to it read aloud? Seeing is not believing when it comes to poetry—hearing is.

When I read Kevin Young's "Mercy," I liked it immediately because it featured a father and mother who were farmers. But it was not until I read the poem aloud that I realized I had misread one word. A tiny preposition—mistaking "in" for "on" —cost me the entire setting of the poem. I initially thought it was set in an airport, but it's in a hospital. It's not like Young left a coded message in his poem. I simply read it too fast. Reading aloud forces me to read more slowly and understand more fully.

Elizabeth Crook is a novelist who was steeped in poetry as a child, and it has affected how she reads and writes. Every night, Elizabeth's mother would read to her and her siblings, prose and poetry, usually for two to three hours. Hearing poetry read taught Elizabeth to read slowly.

"I don't read much faster than I can read aloud," she says. She tried speed-reading classes in high school and college, but she still didn't improve. "The professor asked where I had learned to read, and I told her, 'Sitting on my mom's lap while she read aloud.' 'That's the speed you're reading now,' she said. 'It's not so good for reading most material. It's fine if you're going to be reading poetry.'"

Poetry is not meant to be read with speed. It's meant to be read aloud, with attention and even passion, as Elizabeth reads poems. When I interviewed her, she read several of her favorites from childhood. She said the rhythm and pacing of poetry influences her prose.

"It's more a sense of pacing in the sentence. There's a certain rhythm, a way that words sound together that sticks in your mind and stays with you. I've written lines before and later realized that the line has almost the same rhythm as a poem I knew as a child, the same number of words as some line of poetry that was read to me over and over." Elizabeth further explained, "There's something that hearing poetry all my life gave me that helps me when I'm proofing my own writing by reading it aloud."

Often the end of one of her chapters has "a lot of interior rhyme," but it isn't something she does on purpose. "It just sneaks in."

I interviewed Elizabeth because of a note in the acknowledgments of her novel *Monday, Monday*. She credits two poets who "meticulously combed through the manuscript." One was her sister, Noel Crook, whose newest collection, *Salt Moon*, was published in 2015. The other poet was Timothy McBride, whose collection is *The Manageable Cold*.

"They were extremely helpful to me," Elizabeth said. "They could spot the listless word, the lame description. They could pick out the awkward turns of phrase."

Poets can improve fiction not because they're superior people, but because they immerse themselves in the perfect word, placed in the perfect spot. It's not an unobtainable talent. Anyone who reads poetry daily—especially aloud—can develop it.

At some of her book signings Elizabeth reads a poem to set up the story, which opens with the first mass shooting in a public place at the University of Texas at Austin on August 1, 1966. The poem is from a collection her mother read to her called *All the Silver Pennies*, edited by Blanche Jennings Thompson.

Some One

Some one came knocking
At my wee, small door;
Some one came knocking,
I'm sure—sure—sure;
I listened, I opened,
I looked to left and right,
But nought there was a-stirring
In the still dark night;
Only the busy beetle
Tap-tapping on the wall,
Only from the forest

The screech-owl's call,
Only the cricket whistling
While the dewdrops fall,
So I know not who came knocking,
At all, at all, at all.

—*Walter de la Mare*

I asked her how audiences have responded to this poem.

"I think it sets the mood for the story I'm about to tell, a story about the stranger. I think it explains why I and other writers are drawn to darker themes—the unknown, the unseen, the mysterious that could be evil. It depicts that not only beautifully but visually, accurately."

If I were to read this poem at Halloween, I'd find it delightfully creepy. Reading it as an introduction to a mass murder, it's chilling.

I was introduced to Elizabeth through my dad, whose name is Clif Drummond. She interviewed him on background for *Monday, Monday*. He was student body president of UT at the time of the shooting, and the heroic actions of one of her characters are based on his actions. Dad said that one of Elizabeth's questions about that August day was, "What color was the light?" That's a question only someone thoroughly immersed in poetry would think to ask.

11

Easier Than Giving Up

Writing Poetry

Anyone can write poetry, and most of us have at some point during our academic career. Maybe in middle school we put together a notebook during April, National Poetry Month, following the form explanations our teacher gave us. I support such assignments.

In fifth grade our class published a poetry book called *Pegasus*. No wonder poetry stuck to me like mythological glue. Each chapter featured a type of poetry—cinquain, haiku, senryu, sijo, tanka, and of course, Christmas, which was its own grab-bag of poems loosely surrounding a theme, like the Christmas section of my high school choir closet. I do not remember receiving a grade for this project, only a copy of the book.

It's great that teachers introduce students to forms, but not so great that they grade the poems. If it were up to me, students would write poetry and simply receive a completion grade for doing the work.

After our poetry dare, Nancy Franson contacted me when a friend's son, a high schooler who cared more about baseball than poetry, was given an assignment to write a poem of 15 lines and to include alliteration, assonance, onomatopoeia, repetition, parallelism, portmanteau and enjambment. (Confession: I had to look up *portmanteau*.)

Now, if this same assignment was given at a poetry workshop, the participants' eyes would sparkle, and their No. 2 pencils would scribble with delight. People who love poetry usually love a challenge. But for the love of T. S. Eliot, don't *start* there.

Nancy asked if I'd be okay with mocking the teacher anonymously, "You know, in order to save the children. And the poetry." I was so tempted to mock.

The student completed the assignment and wrote a poem about baseball, adding it to his poetry notebook. The teacher was so impressed she asked if she could keep the notebook to share with future classes, and then she gave him an 85. As Nancy said, "For. The. Love."

It's not hard to love poetry. But it's oh-so-easy to kill that love. Let's teach the writing of poetry better, so this boy and Nancy and baseball fans everywhere can sneak in a poem or two between innings.

When I wrote those poems in fifth grade, my mother already had cancer, although none of my poems are about her. There is one poem by a boy about his brother who died—I don't remember how, but I remember the school assembly when we all observed a moment of silence. I suspect writing the poem was therapeutic for him.

Anyone who writes poetry is familiar with the idea of writing for sanity's sake. Sometimes in a writers' group, when it comes time for a person to read, he or she will say, "This is probably poetry therapy." But that doesn't necessarily mean it's a bad poem. It might be. On the other hand, a lot of great poetry has been written about things that require therapy. What's the difference?

To answer that question, I turned to Lianne Mercer, who is a poet, a retired psychiatric nurse, and a certified poetry therapist.

The National Association for Poetry Therapy has a conference, a website, and a tagline: "Promoting growth and healing through language, symbol, and story." Their mascot is a Pegasus, the mythological symbol of poetry.

Lianne said she became a psych nurse because she "wasn't any good at giving people shots." She had always written poetry and taken writing classes around her nursing schedule, but she didn't begin to write in earnest until a personal loss in midlife.

"Poetry was an outlet, especially when I was getting divorced in '84. Don't you find it's a release of emotion and a way of looking at things in maybe a different way?" she asked.

Yes, Lianne. Yes, I do.

Lianne has led poetry workshops and classes for about 25 years both before and after she became a poetry therapist. Her approach is simple—let's write.

"It doesn't have to be four lines that rhyme," she tells people. "Let's just write poetry."

She focuses on using images to write, especially from childhood. As a personal example, Lianne shares, "For me, it's the fall trees, the leaves on the ground, the burning of the leaves, and how I hated lighting matches and my mother made me so I wouldn't be afraid."

I can't put that image out of my mind—little Lianne, scared to light matches but doing it anyway because her mother made her.

Lianne said sometimes people are afraid to write poetry because they think it has to be good.

"What does that mean? What do they think 'good poetry' means? I don't know what good poetry is," she said, but then she defined it. "To me, good poetry is when my heart beats on the page. I think it's good if it moves you, if it makes you cry, if it makes you laugh, if it makes you say, 'Oh, wow!'"

Lianne said some people write solely for the emotional release and after that they don't care what happens to the words.

"It's using poetry to get in touch with yourself and get in touch with others. It's a way of knowing yourself, I think, and helping others."

It's the writers in her groups who hang onto those words like buoys and revise them endlessly. How much more good poetry might be generated if we didn't endlessly evaluate our efforts— if we wrote and wrote and wrote and got through the bad, the sentimental, the therapeutic and made way for the occasional good poem?

That's what poet Billy Collins thinks, two-time U. S. poet laureate and a genuinely funny fellow. When Collins was the "Not My Job" guest on the NPR game show and podcast *Wait, Wait, Don't Tell Me*, he said everyone is born with 200 bad poems. He suggested the teenage years are a good time to get rid of those. So if you already wrote 200 bad poems in middle school and high school, then it's your time to shine. If you were otherwise engaged, actually living your life, then get busy churning out some awful, schlocky stuff.

Just write. It doesn't have to be good.

Start with "roses are red, violets are blue." That old formula works because it's true. Roses are red, violets are blue. If a poem begins, "roses are yellow, violets are purple," that would be true as well because each of those flowers comes in more than one color. If you were to write, "roses are brown, violets are black," then we'll assume you forgot to water your flowers, and now they're dying, which happens at my house. "Roses are tie-dyed, violets are polka-dotted"—that's full-out surrealist territory. Home run.

Author Ann Patchett tells a story, in her collection of essays *This Is the Story of a Happy Marriage,* about the annual fall softball game at the Iowa Writers' Workshop. The game would set fiction writers against poets.

"The poets always won and the fiction writers never minded. The poets may have had a stronger pitching style, but their lives would be harder," Patchett writes.

Why write poetry? Because poets have perfect pitch.

Perhaps people willing to put in all those hours are those with harder lives, like Patchett's friend Lucy Grealy, whom she met in Iowa. Grealy had cancer before she and Patchett became friends. Patchett believes her friend—the poet with the long, hard cancer journey—was the better writer.

I don't know if poets' lives are always harder. I want that not to be true. But would I have come back to poetry any other way?

Once my mother began to accept that her end was nearing, it was not a surprise to my dad or to me, but it was to many of her friends. They'd seen her through cancer after cancer—surely she'd recover again. Mom had a fantasy that she would convalesce for weeks, and her friends would file into her bedroom one by one. They'd visit and laugh and each one would receive a gift from her closet as a memento. But she went downhill too quickly. On Saturday she gave away one piece of clothing, a jacket to my cousin. Sunday she planned her funeral. Monday she lost her mind.

As the liver stops functioning, it ceases to filter toxins. In liver failure the body is essentially poisoned from within. One of the symptoms is disorientation and confusion.

Last Words

Dad calls at 5 a.m.
"It may be today"
but yesterday she ate cherry pie

today I have an ob/gyn appointment 100 miles away
my blood pressure races
I beg the doctor "My mother is literally on her
    death bed."
She frees me. No charge.
I get home in time, but Mom is not there

in bed. She wanders the house
turns up the heater on this warm March day
sits on the couch and pleasantly inquires
as if she has never met me
never met my sister-in-law
"Are you two sisters?"

Amy takes my hand to hush me
answers: "Yes, ma'am!"

Amy is my sister-in-law, who did treat me like a sister that day
and also that night, when she took me out to dinner and ordered
exactly what I like because I was too upset to make sense of a
menu. A week later, before my mother's funeral, she arranged a
mani-pedi, complete with a glass of white wine.

    When my mother did not recognize me, she was not bitter.
She greeted me as if I were a new friend, one who'd popped in

on a whim. I wish I had kept it together enough to talk with her in her confusion, to see how the conversation might have evolved. She probably would have asked about my family first, my job later, if at all. Surely she would have asked where I go to church. Perhaps not even knowing me, she might have had an encouraging bible verse at the ready, one I might have actually benefited from hearing.

Sally Clark brought the following poem to our writers' group when she was judging a contest. It was the winning entry. When I see the ending, I picture Mom kneeling on hard stone floors, not giving up. At times I found her hopefulness tiring, especially in her 29 emails to friends and supporters. But now I wouldn't change a word. Those emails are puredee Merry Nell. Maybe it was therapeutic for her to write them, to let in as much hope as her tiny stained glass windows would allow.

St. Margaret's Chapel, Edinburgh

A millennium of prayers
Rising on candle smoke
Have blacked the ceiling.
Tiny, stained glass windows
Restrict light, but not hope.
The stone floors are hard,
But easier than giving up.

—*Susanna H. Davis*

12

What I Haven't Done

Poetry and Biography

Thus far, this book contains 28 poems. Are they all true? And if they are, are they factually true or true in the greater sense of Truth? How closely do they follow either my life story or the life story of the poet?

Too often when I hear a poet interviewed, the journalist assumes every word in the poem is biography. If that were true, the poet would have written an autobiography, or at least a memoir. Poetry is not memoir. It's not fiction either. It's shelved in the nonfiction section of the library, but it belongs in its own nook. (Poetry is a nookish sort of place.) Biography and poetry are mysterious friends.

The first time I visited my mother's garden grave, six months after her death on a dreary autumn day, it was draped in purple beautyberry fruit. Mom would've remembered to bring yellow roses, I thought, and then I started to cry uncontrollably. Then it started to rain, not a little bit but a deluge. I ran to the car, supposing those wild berries would have to do.

When I read "Monument" by Natasha Trethewey, former U. S. poet laureate from 2012-2014, I liked it because it reminded me of that day at the graveside.

Monument

Today the ants are busy
        beside my front steps, weaving
in and out of the hill they're building.
        I watch them emerge and—

like everything I've forgotten—disappear
        into the subterranean—a world
made by displacement. In the cemetery
        last June, I circled, lost—

weeds and grass grown up all around—
        the landscape blurred and waving.
At my mother's grave, ants streamed in
        and out like arteries, a tiny hill rising

above her untended plot. Bit by bit,
        red dirt piled up, spread
like a rash on the grass: I watched a long time
        the ants' determined work,

how they brought up soil
        of which she will be part,
and piled it before me. Believe me when I say
        I've tried not to begrudge them

their industry, this reminder of what
        I haven't done. Even now,

> the mound is a blister on my heart,
> a red and humming swarm.

—*Natasha Trethewey*

Ah yes, "this reminder of what/I haven't done." Maybe it's only poets who forget to bring flowers to gravesites.

If I saw ants building a mound on my mother's grave, I would "begrudge them." But the ants aren't what this poem is about. It's about the regret and pain the speaker feels. Her grief is "a red and humming swarm." At my mother's grave, I thought my feelings were nicely buried in an emotional urn, in "the subterranean—a world/made by displacement." But it took absolutely nothing to unearth me, to displace me. My heart was "blurred and waving" as surely as my eyes were blurred from crying, and as surely as my landscape, like the landscape in the poem, was "blurred and waving," too.

Let's consider a problem that often arises when trying to understand a poem. Is the speaker in "Monument" Trethewey, or is it another unidentified voice?

I've heard Trethewey interviewed about the collection in which this poem appears, *Native Guard*. Trethewey did lose her mother, who was murdered by her estranged husband, Trethewey's stepfather. It is possible Trethewey literally went to her mother's untended grave and discovered a swarm of red ants. But does that necessarily mean this poem is autobiographical?

Maybe. Maybe not.

Ultimately, the only way for me to know if the poem is 100 percent accurate would be to ask Trethewey. But as someone who practices poetry, I would never ask. Because fundamentally, I don't care. Of course I care about her story and her mother's, but that's separate from the way I care about the poem.

A poem can be completely factual and still be bad. Or it can grow from a small seed of truth and express greater Truth. When I went looking for "Monument," all I remembered was who wrote it and that it had ants and a mother's grave. The images connected with me because I left my own mother's grave untended. It became about my story, not Trethewey's.

Good poetry reaches beyond biography to touch a reader or to talk about greater things. Jacqueline Woodson's National Book Award-winning memoir in verse, *Brown Girl Dreaming*, is autobiographical—she tells us so. But it's not exhaustive. Each poem is almost a snapshot, deliberately chosen and displayed in a scrapbook in a particular order. The style leaves a lot of her story untold, yet it allows room for her to comment on larger themes, such as racism and U. S. history and religion. Her book belongs in an entirely new section of the library.

Sometimes knowing a poet's biography can get in the way of appreciating a poem. *The Writer's Almanac* describes a reading Robert Frost gave at Bowdoin College in 1974, in which he answered questions about his famous poem "Stopping By Woods on a Snowy Evening" more honestly than he had in previous interviews. It seems that the truth, the whole truth, and nothing but the truth was more than he wanted the world to know.

Frost was essentially broke one December day when he went into town hoping to sell enough bounty from his farm to provide a simple Christmas for his family. He failed. As he neared home, Frost cried right there in the snow. The horse shook its jingle bells, and he pulled it together and drove home.

Few of those facts made it into the poem. Frost could have

written about his failure, but he didn't. He could have written about his despair, but he chose not to. He wrote this poem, one that has always brought me satisfaction.

Poetry has the power to transform the truth. It can obscure facts the poet prefers remain hidden. It can protect people the poet loves. A poem offers protection in a way memoir or creative nonfiction never can. In today's digital climate, where everyone's bio is available with a click, even fiction can be too revealing. But in poetry the poet can be hyperspecific about a moment without revealing too much.

A lot of the poems I wrote during my mother's cancer are both precise and opaque. They grew out of true moments, but they're not enough to reconstruct reality. They're breadcrumbs, left all over the trail of her last three years.

Like the Thanksgiving Day when I yelled at a family member on our way to eat the big holiday meal, I wanted to skip the whole holiday event after my outburst, but I forced myself to carry on for my mother's sake. What if this were her last Thanksgiving? (It wasn't.) She sat beside me at the table, and we talked about trivial things to try to cover the damage I'd done. She ordered a slice of apple pie, handed me an extra fork, and asked if I'd share it with her. It is the only time I said yes when she asked me to share a dessert.

Thanksgiving Pie

On Thanksgiving we share a slice of warm apple pie

her fork goes high
scrapes the crunchy topping doused in caramel

mine scoops out the middle
finds fruit rolled in cinnamon and ginger

We savor each sweet bite, ignore the soggy crust.

I wasn't thinking about cancer that Thanksgiving. All I knew was I did not want to remember my outburst, but I did want to remember our pie. I'm still not ready to talk about what I said. Maybe I never will be. The poem is about overcoming the disaster of the day.

The following poem was written after a tragedy the poet didn't feel ready to talk about. That information is not in the text. But a year or so later, when there was a national tragedy, she reposted the poem on her blog, realizing it might have value for other people in their moments of heartbreak. Maybe they didn't want to talk either. Maybe they were standing in a kitchen, breaking eggs to make a pie.

Fragile

This morning,
I cradle empty eggshells
in the palm of my hand
where they rest:
smooth
fragile
broken.

I touch the points
of their jagged edges

and then
lay them gently
on a soft
white
kitchen
towel.

Midwinter sun
filtered through clouds—
through windowpanes streaked by rain—
sheds muted light
on silent mourning.

—*Ann Kroeker*

The poem makes great use of the sense of touch. It uses words like *cradle*, *palm*, *jagged*, and *soft*. This pain of mourning the poet feels—it's tactile.

The other sense explored is sight, but everything is translucent. The sun is "filtered." The windowpanes, "streaked." The light is "muted." Nothing is clear. When something catastrophic happens, our world becomes unclear. Our glasses are gone. We reach out raw hands to feel our way through.

My favorite part is these three words without any punctuation: *smooth/ fragile/ broken*. Yes, that's how it feels when life cracks.

Poetry is my prescription for adversity. It can touch hidden places in ways prose can't. When I am heartbroken and read a poem that seems to have been written from someone else's dark place, I can sit among the broken eggshells and know I'm not alone. I don't need to know how the eggshells got broken.

13

Undammable Song

Good Versus Bad Poetry

Not long after the day at my mother's graveside, I bought two beautyberry bushes and planted them below my kitchen window. I loved that their purple fruit bloomed in September, when it's still hot and dry. And I've always liked purple. In fifth grade I wore purple so often that Mr. Henry, who drove the school bus, nicknamed me The Queen of Purple.

That fifth grade year, the year after my mother's initial cancer, was the worst in our 39-year relationship.

Back in 1981 cancer was still the C-word. My parents never lied to my brother or me. They gave us age-appropriate information. But I wasn't fooled. I knew cancer killed people. And then, somehow, Mom didn't die. That's what I had prepared for as much as a child could. I felt angry at myself for even considering the possibility of death, and I also felt afraid that she might get sick again. What did I do with those emotions? I took them out on my mother. We had more fights that year than any other. It would have been a bad season anyway, with a fifth grade classroom full of cranky girls and bullying boys and a teacher who tried too hard to be nice. I couldn't cope. I put my mother through unnecessary grief. How do I know this? Because someone mentioned it at the luncheon after her burial.

The burial of her cremains happened six weeks after her memorial service. Dad, aka Mr. Hospitality, threw a luncheon for the 40 or so people who attended. After we ate, he invited everyone to share their Merry Nell memories. Their testimonies, as it were.

It was all fine and dandy and slightly weepy until one of my mother's friends looked at me and my brother and said, "You two put your mother through so much. You don't know how hard she prayed for you."

He and I stared at each other. Did she really say that? An hour after we buried our mother? Of course we knew our mother prayed for us. And no, back then we didn't know what we put her through. We know now. We're parents.

This friend loved my mother, but what she didn't understand —what my brother and I didn't understand until after our mother died—was that growing up with a parent who had cancer affected us. How could it not? And since we were children, we did not always respond well. We were living in two worlds, Cancer World and the real world. One world on land, one underwater. We were like a dipper.

The Dipper

It was winter, near freezing,
I'd walked through a forest of firs
when I saw issue out of the waterfall
a solitary bird.

It lit on a damp rock,
and, as water swept stupidly on,

wrung from its own throat
supple, undammable song.

It isn't mine to give.
I can't coax this bird to my hand
that knows the depth of the river
yet sings of it on land.

—*Kathleen Jamie*

When in doubt about bird behavior, consult the Cornell Lab of Ornithology. Here is its description of the dipper: "A chunky bird of western streams, the American Dipper is North America's only truly aquatic songbird. It catches all of its food underwater in swiftly flowing streams by swimming and walking on the stream bottom."

I had no idea there was such a thing as an aquatic songbird, much less one described as "chunky."

The speaker in the poem saw the bird "issue out of the waterfall." The word *issue* is unexpected, as is seeing a bird walk out of a waterfall. This poem is about a moment of discovery.

But the discovery is not about the waterfall, which is the kind of thing poets usually praise. No, this water "swept stupidly on." Stupid water!

The description of the bird's song isn't pretty. The song is "wrung from its own throat." The word *wrung* is a one-syllable word that carries a lot of weight. It makes me think of wringing a dishcloth or possibly even a neck. What does this bird sing? "Undammable song." The song is "undammable," like the waterfall which cannot be dammed, but I also hear "undamnable." This song cannot be stopped, not even by hell.

The poem ends with the speaker waiting, wanting to learn from this bird that catches its food underwater, in "the depth of the river/yet sings of it on land." One bird. Two worlds.

My mother moved back and forth between two worlds during her 29 years with cancer. My brother and I and my dad learned to move between them, too. We could have all learned a thing or two from this dipper, even if we couldn't coax it to our hands.

"The Dipper" is an example of good poetry. It has rhyme. It's about an unusual subject. It raises deep questions without offering pesky answers. But many people never make it to a good poem like this one because they've read too much of the bad stuff and stopped reading poetry altogether. By bad I mean plain ole bad, like the depressing poetry I wrote in high school.

Every Friday is Haiku Friday at Mark Osler's blog, *Osler's Razor*. Osler is a law professor and a former federal prosecutor, so he gets lots of non-poets writing haiku. That makes the poetry in the comment section unexpected and often funny.

On January 18, 2013, he wrote: "Are you ready for some POETRY? And not just any old poetry—this time we are shooting for ultra-dark, super-depressing poetry of the style you find in high school literary magazines."

Here is the sample he posted:

There's no need to cry
The clouds do it for me
Expressing my depression better
Than I ever could.

Why is this bad poetry? Let me count the ways. And let me use this poem to explain why Jamie's poem is good.

1) It violates the credo "Show, Don't Tell." Don't tell us you're depressed. Show us your depression. But Jamie shows us a person walking through a "forest of firs" in winter, "near freezing," observing "a solitary bird." That's showing. There is feeling in those words, but interpretation is left open.

2) It employs cliché: clouds/rain equals sadness/crying. Cliché has uses. It can work against type, as in "Sunny days make me saddest of all." Jamie's poem does not glorify the water or the bird or its song in the way I might anticipate. It invites me to see the scene in a new way.

3) Other than those poor pathetic clouds, there's no imagery in the bad poem. But when I read Jamie's, my brain composes a mini movie.

4) The poem about depression makes me feel sorry for the writer, although I don't know what to do with my pity. But Jamie's poem doesn't ask for sympathy. The speaker explains the bird has something she doesn't, something that "isn't mine to give." I leave her poem feeling intrigued, not like I'd been handed a guilt trip on a poetic platter.

5) There's little attention to poetic form in the first poem. Even without rhyme, there should be alliteration or internal rhyme or some sort of rhythmic quality. There should be reasons for the line breaks. In Jamie's poem, the second and fourth lines of each stanza rhyme. The first and third lines have echoes of rhyme, a vowel or a consonant or a sound that is repeated.

But in defense of the first poet, I do like that the words *depression better* are smushed together. Can we do "depression better" in poetry? Can we keep genuine sadness from becoming melancholy?

We need what I like to call a *basket*, a concrete image that carries emotional weight without scaring off readers. We need not just any bird but The Dipper. Not just any flower but red poppies.

I finally had to throw away the beautyberry bushes. They survived the multi-year drought but not the spring and summer rain. They caught some kind of fungus and died. I will miss their amethyst fruit under my kitchen window this fall.

John suggested I put down new soil, plant new flowers.

I've never been a gardener, and Mom gardened sporadically, always losing her impatiens to the deer. I bought the beautyberry bushes because they were native plants that wouldn't need work. I'd love to grow wildflowers, but it is in their nature to grow where they are not planted.

At Mile 37

At mile 37 red poppies do abide
near fields of what we think will soon be corn,
past horses pale, their hearts held close inside
thin skin. Today is not a day to mourn
though if I say I am not sad I lied.

You're gone. We rose and took it in our stride.
We pedaled hard and spied white poppies worn
from drought. Until we reached a red clump wide.
At mile 37.

Only then the red blooms promised for our ride,
sought at every pickup truck's loud horn
that blared at us for forty-two May miles,
to the right, beneath a black mailbox beside
the road we found red poppies newly born.
At mile 37.

"In Flanders Fields" by John McCrae is a good poem about red poppies, one that has lasted for 100 years and will probably be recited 100 years from now.

I know nothing of war, little of death. But I know that one sad May day I spent 37 out of 42 miles on a bicycle, winding through towns called Walburg and Weir, searching for red poppies on the Red Poppy Ride. When I finally found them, I wanted to memorialize my search in a poem. Each attempt to write the experience failed, until I attempted to follow the form, a rondeau, used by McCrae. He wrote of the dead of World War I and the fields of blood that later turned into fields of red poppies.

Because of McCrae, for poets, red poppies will never just be wildflowers. They are death and beauty and resilience and sacrifice, blooming wherever they wish. For me, they are also now that sorrowful bike ride and the joy of finally finding the promised flower.

14

Come Night

Old Poetry

Mom was beautiful. Everyone said so. Even on her worst days, she took care to look her best, and she always wore lipstick. So, I think it must have been difficult for her to lose her hair.

I was not there when she had her head shaved. I assumed she'd had it done, since most women who lose their hair due to chemotherapy choose at some point to control the hair loss themselves. But she never admitted it to me. I didn't know for sure that she had shaved her head until my dad mentioned it more than five years after her death. He said he was there and that Mom was surrounded by friends. He described it as a prayer meeting in the beauty salon.

"You look as pretty as ever," he told her when it was finished.

My mother never let me see her bald. She wore her pink Race for the Cure ball cap, the one with so many pink survivor ribbons there was hardly room for them all. I remember her wig —auburn—a color her salt-and-pepper hair never dreamed of. It was the closest she ever came to dying her hair. When her hair did return, it was stark white.

Her hair was always short, and mine looks better short as well. But when my mother was undergoing chemotherapy, I could not bear to snip what she was losing. For more than a year I did not cut my hair. After she died, I still couldn't bring myself to do it. I'd look too much like her, and I felt that I didn't deserve to. I wasn't as tough or as brave or as faithful or as friendly or as hopeful or as beautiful as she was. It took five years for me to summon the courage to cut my hair short. When I did, I went to her hairdresser, who did indeed say, "You look so much like your mom."

I've never enjoyed having my hair washed at the salon, but my mother adored it. For her it was a head massage, the perfect prelude to sitting pretty in the chair.

There was a moment at the end of her life that was not pretty. It took as long for me to come to terms with it—five years —as it did for me to cut my hair short. Finally, it took a poem, an old one, to reframe the moment for me. I looked it up because of something my poetry buddy Nancy Franson said.

Nancy and I were discussing the latest movie version of *Cinderella* on Facebook, and she had an explanation for the wicked stepmother and what she called "her appalling daughters." Nancy wrote, "They probably never had any poetry in their lives."

No, probably not. Imagine how much nicer things might have been for Cinderella if she and her stepsisters had gathered every morning over porridge to read a poem together. They might not have been so bothered about Prince Charming and his silly ball if they had read this poem, which, for reasons I cannot explain, I felt compelled to look up after our discussion.

Pied Beauty

Glory be to God for dappled things–
   For skies of couple-colour as a brinded cow;

For rose-moles all in stipple upon trout that swim;
Fresh-firecoal chestnut-falls; finches' wings;
　Landscape plotted and pieced—fold, fallow, and plough;
　And áll trádes, their gear and tackle and trim.

All things counter, original, spare, strange;
　Whatever is fickle, freckled (who knows how?)
　With swift, slow; sweet, sour; adazzle, dim;
He fathers-forth whose beauty is past change:
　　Praise him.

　　—*Gerard Manley Hopkins*

I tend to have a hard time with old poetry. But a daily diet of a poem with my porridge (oatmeal) has made the older stuff easier to digest. Although occasionally, as with this poem, I have to use a dictionary. According to Webster's *New College World Dictionary, pied* means "covered with patches or spots of two or more colors." It matches other words in the poem that mean essentially the same thing, like *dappled, brinded, stipple,* and *freckled.*

How might Cinderella's life have been different if her step-sisters considered freckled things beautiful? If those young women praised the beauty of cows and trout? If they noticed how lovely farm gear looks in a field? If "All things counter, original, spare, strange" were appreciated? It might have been a very different fairy tale.

I knew Hopkins' poem before our *Cinderella* exchange, but afterward, I printed it to save in my poetry scrapbook. After reading it aloud, I rewrote a poem about an unpretty moment, when my mother's skin had turned yellow from jaundice and was oddly speckled from chemotherapy.

Beauty Shop

The nurse assistant comes to wash the body
in her bed with sterile towels.
"We're going to the beauty shop," she chirps.
"Gonna get you all pretty."

Morning sun streams through windows
there's new evidence of disease.
"You've really been through it, Hon, haven't you?"
The nurse mutters.

She asks me to help her as she sweats
and lifts and turns the almost dead
weight. I am not strong enough. But I notice
when she washes my mom's hair oh!

there is a sound
that happy sound my mother always makes
at the beauty shop. I sigh,
"Mom loved to have her hair washed."

Looking back, I'd call that a moment of pied beauty.

Shortly after the nurse and my dad managed to get her into a clean nightgown, I sat by Mom's bedside, singing to her while she slept. Soon, family from Wyoming came to say their goodbyes. I'd already said mine. I drove home with the sunroof open, letting in the light from the moon and the spring stars.

When I found this poem, it reminded me of my mother's cancer journey and all such journeys that take longer than we think when we begin them.

Up-Hill

Does the road wind up-hill all the way?
   Yes, to the very end.
Will the day's journey take the whole long day?
   From morn to night, my friend.

But is there for the night a resting-place?
   A roof for when the slow dark hours begin.
May not the darkness hide it from my face?
   You cannot miss that inn.

Shall I meet other wayfarers at night?
   Those who have gone before.
Then must I knock, or call when just in sight?
   They will not keep you standing at that door.

Shall I find comfort, travel-sore and weak?
   Of labour you shall find the sum.
Will there be beds for me and all who seek?
   Yea, beds for all who come.

—*Christina Rossetti*

Occasionally, *Every Day Poems* features old poems, like this one. One December when they featured several around the theme of "Nightie Night" and, unofficially, Christmas, I found myself enjoying the old rhymes and rhythms more than I expected, perhaps because Christmas and Nightie Night are themes I can grasp without assistance. Maybe it took old poetry to carry the weight of my loss.

from Romeo and Juliet, Scene III, Act II

Come, night, come, Romeo, come, thou day in night;
For thou wilt lie upon the wings of night
Whiter than new snow on a raven's back.
Come, gentle night, come, loving, black-brow'd night,
Give me my Romeo; and, when he shall die,
Take him and cut him out in little stars,
And he will make the face of heaven so fine
That all the world will be in love with night
And pay no worship to the garish sun.

—*William Shakespeare*

My favorite lines are "Take him and cut him out in little stars,/And he will make the face of heaven so fine/That all the world will be in love with night." It's a graphic image but a lovely one. What if the stars were the faces of our long-gone loved ones? Then I would want it to be night all the time, to see Mom sparkle-ate. (I know that's not a word, but I wrote it in my poetry journal early one morning under the stars.)

Not long after she died, Dad gave me a glass starfish. It's about the size of my hand and heavy. Because of the way it's cut, the starfish appears different colors in different lights, and it changes color depending on whatever I set it upon. I've made it glow blue, red, pink, yellow, even green when I hold it up to the sun. When I started this project I moved it from my bedside table to my writing pile. Sometimes it sits on my purple three-ring binder, where I collect poems. Other times I lay it on my gray notebook, where I write poetry early in the morning. I want Mom's star with me all the time, bringing day in night.

15

There Will Never Be Enough

Poetry of the Crisis

My mother's cancer journey was long, but her experience is less uncommon than it used to be. For many people, cancer is a chronic condition. It flares up. It gets treated. I wish for all of these people 29 years and many more.

Although those extra years took a toll on our family, we made the most of them. During the first summer after my mother's cancer came back, when she still felt good, Mom and Dad traveled all over the country, visiting beaches and mountains and friends. They celebrated their 40th anniversary as if it were their 50th. Their clock unwound its tune to 43-and-a-half years, almost exactly.

And I wouldn't trade her last three years, not only because we had more time together, time to get to know each other as adults, woman to woman, but also because the only way I could cope with her cancer was to write poetry. I don't know if I'd be writing poems today without her extra years of suffering. I do know I needed every single day she gave me.

I would prefer that she were still here. She would say it is enough that her suffering gave rise to something that saved me. She was the kind of parent who would give her life for her child.

I didn't know that poetry—reading and writing it—would serve me well in hard times to come. I wish losing my mother was the last rotten wind to blow through my life, but no. There have been other deaths, other tragedies. I've had poetry for every crisis.

In *Poetry at Work*, Glynn Young has a chapter called "The Poetry of the Crisis." He writes,

> It's difficult to see when you're in the thick of a crisis, but you can look for the poetry that's there, because it is there. You can see it in the themes, the metaphors, the rhythm and flow, what words are used and how they are used. And finding the poetry in the crisis will suggest the path forward.

One day, I'd planned to cheer myself by going out to lunch, but the spot I'd picked suddenly closed due to a health crisis in the family. There in the parking lot I checked my email, and a friend had written to check on me. I told her about the restaurant closing and about how petty I was acting about it. Even though she lives more than 1,000 miles from me, she went online and looked up every single sandwich shop in my small city and sent me a list. She also sent me that day's selection from *Every Day Poems*, saying, "I felt you in this poem."

The Woman at the Stoplight

I see in her face
that oh, she needs it too—

a gap in the day,
cloistered though not

confining,

person-
sized pocket to slip into,

buffered as by a cloud's
sheer inner lining,

for a breath
of self-replenishment,
self-repair,

or only just
a breath,
(stanza break)

and then
(I promise!)
out again,

far from too much
to ask,

so with the full force
of my small ferocity,

I importune the air:

"What would it cost
you who are only

lavish, seamless,

great incorporeal sprawl
of everywhere?—

open!
And admit us."

—*Claire Bateman*

Yes, I needed "a gap in the day," "a breath/of self-replenishment,/ self-repair," and my friend knew it. She used "the full force/ of [her] small ferocity" to make sure the world opened to me and I got a sandwich. As I ate, as I read, the poetry admitted me. It was the perfect "(stanza break)" from my crisis.

This is what I know to be true—I live in a body that needs sandwiches, especially during a crisis. I also need poetry, its themes and metaphors, its rhythm and flow, what words are used and how, as Glynn Young said. Poetry was and is my path forward.

I've known people who, after losing someone, turned to poetry even though they'd never read or written it outside of a classroom. Somehow nothing else seemed strong enough to carry their emotions and move them along.

The day after my mother died, I swam at the gym's indoor pool. There was a whiteboard with instructions for the master's swim class, which met pre-dawn. I turned those words into what's called a "found poem," meaning the poet found the words laying around, minding their own business, and stole them. The title alone is mine.

Instructions for Grieving

Look down
Lean in
Pierce the water
Soften your recovery
Move silently as you can
Cut a hole with your fingertips
Find your bliss

A year after my mother's death, Dad and I went to Big Bend National Park. Of all the trips the two of them took together, this was the one they never quite got around to making. We saw a very different section of the Rio Grande as it ran between Texas and Mexico, yet Boquillas Canyon also resembled the cliffs around Creede. While we were there at dusk, the color of the cliffs changed four times in the setting sun, from brown to gold to red to grey.

The same Rio Grande, like in Creede, and yet unlike. I'd stood in the mouth of the Rio Grande holding a fishing pole at Creede in 2008. Here I was in 2011, where the river bends, holding a camera. In Creede, the water was cold. In Boquillas, it was warm. In Creede, deep and powerful. In Boquillas, shallow and quiet.

It is possible to travel the length of the Rio Grande. A couple of journalists with *The Texas Tribune* did it in 2014-2015, from the San Juans to the Gulf Coast. It required all kinds of permissions to cross all sorts of borders. The watercrafts they used were small and agile, nothing like the ship of grief I seemed to be building.

In the Low Countries

They are building a ship
in a field
much bigger than I should have thought
sensible.
When it is finished
there will never be enough of them
to carry it to the sea
and already it is turning
rusty.

—*Stuart Mills*

This is one of the poems Lemony Snicket included in his children's poetry portfolio. He focused on the word *sensible*. In a crisis we need sensible people, those who keep their heads and do what needs to be done, stitch wounds or distribute bottled water. That is one way to survive.

There is another way, one that looks as foolish as building a ship in a field. In the movie *Silver Linings Playbook*, Tiffany takes the money she receives from her deceased husband's life insurance policy and builds a small dance studio in her parents' detached garage. It's completely impractical. She's not even a dancer. But she needs to dance. Dancing is her ship.

Writing poetry is mine. I write in every crisis. Some of those poems will surely rust and perish in forgotten green spiral notebooks. It is enough to write them.

16

In the Wake of Our Sleep

Poetry and Dreams

I've been troubled by bad dreams for most of my life. I don't have trouble going to sleep; it's that I don't like what I find while I'm there. When I was about seven years old, before my mother's cancer, I had the same nightmare every night involving the wolf from Beatrix Potter's *The Tale of Jemima Puddle-Duck* and the sky falling. I was Chicken Little, forced to choose—hungry wolf in a cave or the open air and heavens crumbling.

Perhaps I would have been less scared of that recurring dream if I'd read this poem from Rudyard Kipling's *The Jungle Book*. Since it did not appear as a song in the 1967 Disney movie, I didn't recognize it when it showed up at *Every Day Poems*.

Seal Lullaby

Oh! Hush thee, my baby, the night is behind us,
    And black are the waters that sparkled so green.
The moon, o'er the combers, looks downward to
      find us
    At rest in the hollows that rustle between.
Where billow meets billow, there soft be thy pillow;
    Ah, weary wee flipperling, curl at thy ease!
The storm shall not wake thee, nor shark

> overtake thee,
>
> Asleep in the arms of the slow-swinging seas.

—Rudyard Kipling

Asleep on the "slow-swinging seas"—sounds nice, right? Until I thought about it. I want to go to sleep *beside* the slow-singing seas, on a beach towel laid over the warm sand at South Padre. Asleep *on* the slow-swinging seas? No, thank you. Then I read the poem again. This lullaby is full of things that aren't particularly sleep-inducing. The green water looks black in the dark. There are storms. There are even sharks. Sleep is scary for a lot of children and even, occasionally, for adults. I think Kipling has written the best possible lullaby, one that acknowledges the terrors of night.

For the first few months after my mother died, I dreamed about her often. In the first dream I was at a shopping mall (who goes to malls anymore?), and Mom passed me. She didn't say anything. She just looked at me and smiled, as if to say she was fine, she was just checking up on me. That dream was okay.

But there was another not long after that haunted me for weeks. I dreamed I was at my parents' house, after Mom's death. It was evening. I was clearing away drinks and snacks from a party, when she appeared, smiling.

"What are you doing here?" I asked.

"Didn't you know?" she answered. "I was healed!"

"But there was a funeral. I was there," I told her. "Everyone was."

All she did was smile.

I woke up panicked, unsure whether she was dead or alive. I pulled out her obituary, which I had written. I flipped through the stack of sympathy cards. Yes, she had to be dead. I remembered how in the Sunday school room where the family gathered before we processed down the center aisle for her memorial service, some health-conscious Austinite put out a giant bowl of fresh berries—blackberries, strawberries, raspberries, blueberries. I didn't dream berries.

Maybe if I had written a poem about that sweet fruit, then "night's worry" would not have trailed me, as it does the speaker in this poem.

What Lives in the Wake of Our Sleep

I dream of peaches on the tree by the river,
of my youngest son lost along its muddy banks.

When I wake night's worry trails me to the bathroom
and later to the breakfast table. It is winter here

and the tree is bare. The peaches wait in the freezer
until my wife thaws them for cobbler. Each morning

my boy climbs the black steps of the school bus
and leaves me to what lies in the loose folds

of these sheets: the bed unmade, the mud untracked.

—*Todd Davis*

This is a poem about dreams, about "What Lives in the Wake of Our Sleep." The speaker's dream is of peaches but also of a son.

The boy isn't literally lost, but he is growing up. He "climbs the black steps of the school bus" and leaves. Until I read that line, I'd never thought about how the steps of the school bus are black. And look at what is left behind: "the bed unmade, the mud untracked." Two un's in a row. *Unhappy.*

Meanwhile, "The peaches wait in the freezer."

I can't read a poem that mentions peaches without thinking of the line "Do I dare to eat a peach?" from T. S. Eliot's poem "The Love Song of J. Alfred Prufrock." Is this poem an allusion to that one? I don't know. Some poets spend a great deal of time on allusions—Eliot was one of them—and some work hard to avoid them. Allusions can add another layer to a poem. Or they can feel like an unnecessary intrusion.

The speaker in Davis' poem doesn't need a dare to eat a peach. He wants the peaches, but they are temporarily unattainable, frozen, waiting to be made into cobbler. There is a time to eat peaches, in summer, the season associated with the carefree days of childhood. This poem takes place in winter; the peach tree is bare. In order to enjoy the fruit again, out of season, it will need to be transformed into cobbler. Likewise, in order to recapture the joyous days of childhood, the fruit will need to take a new form.

Believe me, I know this. My kids are in their late teens. The school bus is long gone. The fruit is no longer raw and fresh but mixed with other ingredients into a wholly new substance. Yes, eating a peach might be a daring activity after all.

After my nightmare about my mother, I got stuck in another round of bad dreams. Not all were about her, but her death seemed to open a channel to a river with "muddy banks." There are pills to help a person go to sleep and pills to help a person stay asleep. I have not found a pill that bestows good dreams. For that I needed *Harry Potter.*

I listened to one chapter a night from all seven audiobooks in J. K. Rowling's series. It took about nine months to finish them. English actor Jim Dale reads the unabridged audiobooks and does all the voices. He's stunning. You might think listening to *Harry Potter* every night would interrupt my dreams. It did. That was the whole point—better dreams. It worked. It also brought me back to writing poetry.

For me, there seems to be a perfect amount of tension needed to write poems. Too little stress, and I'm swimming along, oblivious to beauty and wonder. Too much, and I cannot see any connections. Life is ugly, random. During the last stage of my mother's cancer, I was not her caregiver; Dad was. I popped in and out once a week for three years, so my stress level was manageable. After she died, I was like the "bed unmade" in Davis' poem. I didn't write more poetry until after my sojourn with Harry.

I've always been amazed by a poem's power to do great things with few words, as if it could cast spells. But for months when I would swing my poetry wand, it did not even let off sparks. Somehow listening to *Harry Potter* for approximately 270 nights repaired my poetry wand. I'm not sure why it worked, although the idea of Platform 9 3/4 is fertile ground for poetry. The idea that things like boarding school and celebrity authors and even prejudice can be rendered imaginatively—pure poetry grist. Perhaps better dreams are part of the secret to writing poetry.

Toward the end of listening to the series I went to the grocery store and bought a new 6-by-9-inch spiral notebook with a cover the color of a Creede, Colorado, summer sky. I also bought a new package of Sharpwriter No. 2 pencils. That's all I needed to make a little magic. I started noticing things again, things as simple as peaches. (I live in peach country.)

Those who have read the *Harry Potter* books or seen the movies have heard the word *horcrux*. A horcrux is an object in which a slice of someone's soul is hidden. It's an evil thing that can only be created in conjunction with murder.

There was no murder in my mother's death. But if it's true that as most women age we find ourselves becoming more like our mothers, this truism is compounded when a mother dies. There is this void in the cosmos, and the person who can best hold the dead person's sliver of soul is the person most like the mother: her daughter. And yet.

I am not like my mother. She was a bible study teacher, but I write and edit for a magazine. She adored her poodles until her kids were born, but my kids have never lived in a house without at least one dog. I like to ride my bicycle for three-hour jaunts, but her idea of a good bike ride was pedaling down the street in a Fourth of July parade.

This round and round thinking, the repeated "she but I" refrain, this calls for a sestina.

A sestina is a form poem that repeats the same six words, in a rolling fashion, at the end of the lines. Sestinas are good for questions, mysteries, or Escher-drawing-like-experiences in which the proverbial stairs simultaneously go up and down. Unlike most of my poems about my mother, which I worked and reworked right up until publication, this one came out whole and remains unchanged.

Who Am I?

"Let's go for a walk,"
she'd say, and then my mother
would circle the block. I'd question
why we couldn't go farther. My body
could handle it. But Merry
Nell's couldn't. She needed a horcrux

or, perhaps, more than one horcrux.
To figure that out, she'd need a longer walk
through the neighborhood. She'd be merry,
as she always was. I am a mother
who likes to push her body.
There's no question

about it. But every day I question
why I am her horcrux.
Why everybody seems to think that I am walking her
    walk,
that I am mothering like my mother.
It's true. My name is also Merry,

and I also chose to marry
at 21. That is not the question.
I need to know how to mother
without one. All I have is a horcrux,
one I bring with me each morning I take a walk:
my own body.

But it's acting strangely, my body.
It's giving me signs, as yours did, Merry
Nell. Oh, it still can walk
up actual mountains. But I do question
because it doesn't feel like mine. It feels like a horcrux.
I feel like I am you, my dear, dead mother.

And I'm not, am I? Holy Mary, mother
of God. Pray. You're not here in body.
Neither is my mom. She's only a horcrux.
She wasn't into you, Mary. She didn't even have a question
about you. Not even when she couldn't walk.

Like Harry, I am the horcrux. I am not my mother.
I can still walk, and I still dwell in this body.
But I am Merry Megan. No question.

—*(Merry) Megan Willome*

17

For Nothing

Why Poetry?

No, I am not my mother. Guess who is? My daughter—even though she is not named for my mother but for *her* mother, my grandmother.

A few months before Mom died, I sent her a card in which I said that when she was gone, I would simply look at my daughter, mini Merry Nell, and then I would miss her a little less. That's because my mother's personality genes skipped me and found my daughter.

When I was a teenager, I swore—like all teenage daughters everywhere—that I would grow up to be nothing like my mother. And I did grow up to be very different. Once I was a mother of a daughter, I began to wish that at least a few of Mom's traits had made it to me. I am glad my daughter had her example for almost 11 years.

During that decade, I watched them bond as they cuddled on the sofa, reading. Or my daughter would sit in my mother's bathroom, watching her put on makeup, as Mom explained each item's purpose and proper application. (My daughter would never learn that information from me; I don't wear makeup.) Each summer, my daughter would go to Mom's house for a week and do Camp Ama, which was the grandma camp my mother did especially for her.

No wonder that at my mother's funeral, my daughter, then a fifth-grader, gave a eulogy. She read from a book by Doris Stickney called *Water Bugs and Dragonflies: Explaining Death to Young Children* that Mom had given to her. She read clear and strong, without a trace of self-consciousness. She was in complete control of that audience of 500-plus people. No one seems to remember anything about my mother's funeral except my daughter reading from that book.

The book is not a poem. It's a simple story. But it works the way a poem does, drawing on imagination. It asks the reader to imagine that death is like transforming from a water bug into a dragonfly.

Mom's funeral included prose—bible readings and stories about Merry Nell. It also included something almost but not quite entirely like a poem. That's what everyone remembers.

What if there were no poetry? What if all life were prose?

Some people wouldn't mind. One friend told me her son didn't know how to do imaginative play. He lined up his action figures and then shrugged and walked away. He didn't know what else to do. Poetry gives you an idea of what to do, or at least the idea that something more *can* be done. Poetry gives you the confidence to imagine action figures rescuing a dolphin trapped on an ancient version of Mars, with water. Or something even wilder.

Why poetry? For its limitations. Whether a poem is following a form or whether it's expressing an idea or a story in a condensed format, its narrowness gives breadth. A sestina, with its particular repetition of end words, frees the poet to say things he or she might not be able to say in straight prose. Theater works this way as well. There are things that can be done on a stage that can't be done on film. The imagination of the audience is as essential as the lighting, especially in a play like *Our Town* by Thornton Wilder, which has little set or scenery.

Or I can hear one song, "Ring of Keys," from *Fun Home*, which won Best Musical at the Tony Awards in 2015. Almost everything about my life and experience is different from that of Alison Bechdel, whose 2006 graphic memoir is the basis for the musical. But I identify with a girl, Small Alison, trying to figure out who she is.

That unexpected kinship also happens when I read poetry.

Why poetry? For kinship. I am a white woman, but there is something in Juan Felipe Herrera's "Half Mexican" that resonates with me. It's a poem about identity—the eternal "Who am I" question, which I have not only asked but written about in my horcrux poem. Einstein is in Herrera's poem, as is Kant, as are pyramids and quarks. I have no experience with any of those things. I still love it.

I also love it because Mom would be thrilled that Herrera was named the first Latin-American U. S. poet laureate. She might not know any of his poetry, but if she were here, she'd be calling me to make sure I knew about his appointment. And if she heard Herrera doing an on-air interview, she might call in for the opportunity to speak Spanish with him.

Why poetry? For delight. Because it pops up in unexpected places, like in the middle of my yoga class when our teacher said, "The hips are the orchestra. They're down in the pit. That's where all the action is." I did not find this poetic metaphor baffling but immediately began to move my hips in a more orchestra-like fashion. "And the shoulders are the balcony," she added. "Bring them in line over the orchestra."

Now I no longer think about the prose of having good posture. Instead I think about lining up my balcony over my orchestra.

Why poetry? For specificity. Kathleen Jamie's poem I discussed earlier is called "The Dipper." It's not "The Sparrow" or "The Eagle" or "The Grackle." Just reading those alternate titles brings to mind completely different themes that are suggested by those specific birds.

Maybe you're a writer who falls into the trap of using the same word over and over. A writer friend who read an early draft of this manuscript later used the word *apothecary* in an unusual way in her column I was editing. She wasn't talking about an actual apothecary, those shops of old that peddled something between pharmaceutical potions and snake oil. She was discussing advertising, in which sneaker companies sell both shoes and speed.

"It was a wild card use, right?" she emailed. "But that's been a benefit of reading your book. I've been thinking about word use so much more. You forget how powerful the individual words can be. And poets obviously never lose sight of that."

Why poetry? You might as well ask *why chocolate*? Why drive along a country road on a sunny day with the windows down and the music up? Why green tea with fresh mint from the farmer's market? Why dogs?

What if we plunged into poetry the way the dogs in the following poem "plunge straight into/The foaming breakers"? What if we pursued "pleasure/More than obedience"? What if we let the words "toss" us? What if we entered with "absolute innocence/In which we forget ourselves"?

The Dogs at Live Oak Beach, Santa Cruz

As if there could be a world
Of absolute innocence
In which we forget ourselves

The owners throw sticks
And half-bald tennis balls
Toward the surf
And the happy dogs leap after them
As if catapulted—

Black dogs, tan dogs,
Tubes of glorious muscle—

Pursuing pleasure
More than obedience
They race, skid to a halt in the wet sand,
Sometimes they'll plunge straight into
The foaming breakers

Like diving birds, letting the green turbulence
Toss them, until they snap and sink

Teeth into floating wood
Then bound back to their owners
Shining wet, with passionate speed
For nothing,
For absolutely nothing but joy.

—*Alicia Ostriker*

Why poetry? For nothing.

Here's a secret: Poetry is useless. So are a lot of wonderful things—"wet sand," "half-bald tennis balls," "green turbulence."

We don't *need* poetry. Which is exactly why we need it.

18

But Wait

Poetry and Charlotte

I have two dogs, sisters, terrier mixes who were dumped on a ranch. We adopted them seven months before my mother died, and bringing them into our home felt like an affirmation that life would go on. Might as well add puppies, which my kids had been begging for since that trip to Creede.

Most mornings I walk those dogs and then read a poem and try to write one. If nothing comes to mind, I pay attention and then write what I see, what I hear, what the morning feels like, the taste of my tea. Or I write about the book I just read or those century plants suddenly popping up all over town.

If I'm still stuck, I do laundry.

The cure for writer's block

is laundry.
Cram both arms with dirty clothes and
stuff them in the washer.
Brim the detergent, vinegar, bleach, if you dare.
Sit back down.
Write a bit more.
In thirty minutes or an hour, the dinger will ding.
Heap the wet mess into the dryer,

but wait.
The dryer is already packed because you forgot
to fold the last load. Divest the dryer.
Fold the clean clothes, arrange them into piles:
one for him, with you beside him (where you always are),
one for the son, one for the daughter —
the closest they will ever be is these towering piles
of bras, boxers, T-shirts, jeans, uniforms.
Now the dryer is void. Fill it.
Sit down again.
Write.
When the dinger dings, ignore it.
Write on.
Forget to clear the dryer.

Poetry doesn't have to be hard. It can be about dogs or flowers or life or death or pigs or laundry. It can be fun or weird or life-changing. It can be old or modern, have form or float around.

Nancy Franson, my poetry buddy, is as much a part of my poetry journey as my mother, although neither woman intended to steer me in that direction. It all started when Nancy wrote, "Poetry scares me," on Facebook. I took it as a dare—my first poetry dare— and wrote a column for her to celebrate National Poetry Month. My column was about E. B. White's *Charlotte's Web* and the poetry in it. I pointed out that Charlotte saves Wilbur using only five words: *some pig, terrific, radiant,* and *humble.* If that's not poetry, I don't know what is.

Since then, Nancy and I have shared a bit of a writer's crush on E. B. White. In addition to his well-known children's stories (including one about a mouse that might have been an older brother figure for Frederick), he also wrote poems. He co-authored the writer's bible, *The Elements of Style*, better known as "Strunk & White." He wrote essays for *The New Yorker* for six decades. Nancy gifted me a collection of his essays on dogs titled, fittingly, *E. B. White on Dogs*. It re-introduced me to what I believe is the best essay of all time, "Death of a Pig."

White wrote the essay in 1948. It's about, well, the death of a pig. You can't accuse the man of burying the lede. The essay ends with White and his dog Fred standing over the pig's grave. Although the pig died for reasons never fully understood, just a few years later, in 1952, White wrote about another pig, one who lived. That pig was Wilbur. Saved first by Fern and then by Charlotte.

Ever since I first read *Charlotte's Web* as a child, I've kind of liked spiders. Even scary-dangerous ones must be treated with care because, in my mind, they are all distantly related to Charlotte, of whom White wrote at the end of his American fairy tale, "It is not often that someone comes along who is a true friend and a good writer. Charlotte was both." After reading my column, Nancy, who is also a true friend and a good writer, re-read *Charlotte's Web* and sent me an email.

"Guess what I'm reading," she wrote. "I can't believe how beautifully it is written. Thank you so much for recommending I reread it. Not everyone has such a faithful friend who is also a poet. I have both. And I am tremendously blessed."

What is it about poetry that fosters friendship? My mother and I grew closer by reading a story with poetry in it, as did Nancy and I. Any friend who sends me a poem immediately becomes a closer friend. And among my friends who write poetry, like Sally Clark, any differences in our backgrounds or opinions evaporate when we share poems. Something happens when a couple of people come together over a few words.

After Nancy reread *Charlotte's Web*, I did, too. There were times I did not like Wilbur. He was whiny and needy and didn't seem to appreciate the friend he had in Charlotte until she was gone. She was the hero of the story. Despite the rat Templeton's shenanigans, despite Fern's growing up and abandoning her barnyard friends for Henry Fussy, despite her own impending death, Charlotte kept writing.

When her eggs finally hatched, three of her daughters stayed. One was named Joy.

How to Keep, Save & Make Your Life with Poems

For more exposure to poetry and poetic things, visit **Tweet speakPoetry.com** every weekday and subscribe to their newsletter, which comes on the weekend. There will be poetry reviews, poetry prompts, Top 10 lists, infographics on how to write poems, interviews with poets, writing workshop opportunities, and general poetry mischief, including dares. *Tweetspeak* is that rare website where the comments are actually worth reading—it's where all the cool poems hang out. (And the cool poets too.) Also check out the titles from T. S Poetry Press, especially *How to Read a Poem* and *How to Write a Poem*, both by Tania Runyan in conjunction with a famous Billy Collins poem, for more in-depth practice in poetry.

Here are a few other suggestions about how to develop a relationship with poetry, either alone or with others. Each method yields different fruits.

How to Keep a Poetry Journal (As an Individual)

Yes, of course I keep a poetry journal. I have since 2002.

If you are a writer, perhaps you find back-to-school season as thrilling as I do—whole aisles full of notebooks and spirals and composition books and every flavor of pen and pencil. Of course, you can journal digitally, with the electronic device of your choice. But when it comes to poetry, I am old-school.

Materials List

- 3-ring binder
- sheet protectors
- spiral or composition notebook or a nice Moleskine® if you like leather
- pen or pencil
- alternate: The most expensive laptop on the market (if you need justification for such a purchase)

My poetry journal has two parts: the poems I collect and the poems I journal about. Those may be one and the same, but occasionally I print a poem that is so perfect I can't think of anything to write about it. All I can do is read it aloud and sigh with pleasure.

I start a new poetry journal every year right after Thanksgiving, which is my personal end-of-the-year celebration. On that Thursday or maybe the day before or the day after, depending on our holiday plans, I brew a pot of tea and reread all the poems I've collected over the previous 12 months. The collection inevitably becomes a commentary on the year.

I do look over the poems as the year unfolds, too, maybe on a lazy Sunday afternoon, or maybe when I feel a case of writer's block coming on. Poetry usually clears that right up.

How do I choose which poems to print? Simple. They're the ones I like. I print the poem and put it in a sleeve protector in the 3-ring binder. Sometimes I write out the poem in longhand—that's something I should do more often. I have one poem in 2015's journal by Naomi Shihab Nye that was printed in *Texas Monthly*, so I ripped it right out of the magazine.

I use the spiral and my favorite pencil, a No. 2 Papermate Sharpwriter, for journaling about poems.

If you've never journaled about poetry before, I suggest you start by taking one month, 30 days, and do it every day. It will establish the habit and help you learn what you're looking for. Either use the poem from a subscription service (*Every Day Poems* from *Tweetspeak Poetry* is a great place to start) or read through a poetry collection. I'm currently going through the one Elizabeth Crook recommended from her childhood, *All The Silver Pennies*.

How to Journal About a Poem

1) Read the poem silently. Then, read it aloud. Maybe write it out.

2) Now, for the journaling part. What do you think? Was there a phrase you liked? An image that captured your imagination? An amusing rhyme? An unexpected turn?

3) Don't worry about what the poem means—no one knows what it means, often not even the poet, so don't worry about getting it right or wrong. Do you find meaning in the poem? Fabulous! Write it down.

4) If you have a little poetry knowledge, don't be afraid to use it. If you're reading a sonnet, ask yourself whether it strictly follows sonnet form, or if it breaks it, why? Does that improve the poem or make it frustrating? If you can't remember anything from your last poetry unit in middle school, then ignore this paragraph. No worries.

5) Let your mind wander as you write. Did the poem remind you of a memory? Did it make you think of a book you've read or a song you've heard? Did the speaker's voice sound like someone you know? Did it offer comfort or insight into a particular situation in your life? Or—and this is just as valid a response—do you leave the poem wondering, "What was that all about?" Does it go in the category of Not For Me?

6) When you read a Not For Me poem, don't chide yourself and think, "If only I had an MFA, then I'd appreciate it." When you don't like a movie, surely you don't lament the fact that you didn't attend film school, do you? You don't swear off movies forever. Likewise, don't quit poetry altogether. Shrug and move on to the next one.

7) Once you get more familiar with poems, you'll become more familiar with individual poets and may want to check out a collection of their poetry. If the collection is constructed as a unit and not a best-of compilation, the poems will comment on each other. That leads to a different type of journaling, more in-depth.

This may sound like work, but it only takes about 10-15 minutes for me to journal about a poem. Reading a poem a day will take less than a minute. If you read a poem twice, that's two minutes. Read it with your morning coffee or before going to bed. Read it wearing pajamas or a suit or workout gear or jeans and a T-shirt. You need not apply makeup beforehand or bother to tie your shoelaces. The goal of reading a poem a day is to demystify poetry and weave it into your daily life.

These suggestions are simple ideas to get you thinking. Don't feel like you need to answer every question I've listed here. If you spy your own wild hare, by all means chase it.

For the last several years, I've kept my journals separate from the poems themselves. That's because I can get very personal in my commentary on a poem. But now I sometimes combine my words with the poet's. I prefer to write in a spiral with perforated pages that I can easily tear out. Into the sleeve protector it goes along with the poem.

Recently, I looked over the poems in my very first journal. The first one I ever printed was "The Mercy" by Philip Levine. *The Writer's Almanac* featured it on December 1, 2002, and again on November 25, 2003. The way I count time—Thanksgiving to Thanksgiving—that meant "The Mercy" was both the first and last poem in my inaugural journal. If you get into poetry, I promise you'll find coincidences of your own.

How to Be a Poetry Buddy (With a Friend)

Everything I just described? You can do this with a friend. You can share poems with each other. You can share your poetry journals.

When Nancy Franson became my poetry buddy, we were already close friends. We knew without having to ask how a particular poem might hit the other one. When Laura Lynn Brown and I buddied up, we were friends who didn't know each other very well, but we had both lost our mothers. That shared experience plus a love of poetry was enough for us to buddy up.

My buddying with Nancy took place in the summer and fall of 2013, and my buddying with Laura was in spring and summer of 2014. Both exchanges lasted about four months. In Laura's case, that's how long it took to get through the poetry collection we chose, Kevin Young's *Book of Hours*. In Nancy's case, I ended it before I went into a busy season at work. Although I no longer correspond with either buddy daily on poems, when we do, we immediately connect at a deeper level because of our shared journey.

It does not matter where you are in your poetry journey. Nancy and I were paired because I had a level of comfort with poetry, and she was scared of it. That's a valid way to choose a buddy—find someone who already likes poetry and see if they might be interested in buddying with you. Or those of you who already love to discuss poems, reach out to someone who seems to be lurking, waiting to be called on even as they fear they have nothing to say. Perhaps you and a friend both like poetry, but your friend raves about Emily Dickinson, and you think, as I have many times, "I really wish I appreciated Dickinson's poems more, but I need help." Perfect buddy material.

A caution: This technique works well for short poems. Many older poems are longer, more ballad-like. I've never focused on these before. Perhaps a poem like William Cullen Bryant's "Thanatopsis" or Edgar Allan Poe's "The Raven" would require a week. For poems like those, written in language unfamiliar to my 21st century Texan ear, I like to bring in a little art—a good audio recording or a well-illustrated version or even a video. I did not love Walt Whitman's "When I Heard the Learn'd Astronomer" until I saw the *Breaking Bad* clip of the poem on YouTube.

I've done my buddying by email, but if you live in the same city as your buddy, you could gather once a week for tea and toast. Or you could buddy over on the phone or Skype or Voxer. Poetry can work with any technology or in the most low-tech manner possible.

How to Do a Poetry Dare (With a Community)

My dare with Nancy was public; my dare with Laura was private. *Tweetspeak* asked Nancy and me to dare, and we did. In Laura's case, *Tweetspeak* issued a general dare for National Poetry Month, and Laura and I accepted.

The good thing about the public dare was that Nancy and I were each asked to write about our experiences. In other words, there were stakes. We knew that whatever we read and whatever we shared together in the sacred space of email would eventually be shared with the whole world (i.e. the *Tweetspeak* community). I think that made us both work harder. I was thinking not only, "Where is this particular poem and my thoughts about it going?" but also, "Where is this dare going in general? What am I learning? Could any of it help someone else?" The community element not only helped to synthesize my thoughts about a poem but also invited the thoughts of other poetry people, who left comments.

If you're daring with another writer, then you could publish your conclusions at each other's blogs. Or post a number of times, at the beginning, middle and end of your dare. You could seek participation from others as well and expand your poetry community and your poetry appreciation.

The dare is about trying something new, about being willing to learn, and about getting to know people better through poetry. Go ahead, dare. Keep, save, and make your life with poems.

Notes

Chapter 2

page 19   "Another term we like is 'champions' because victory over adversity is implied...": Merry Nell Drummond, personal correspondence, December 28, 2008.

page 20   "Paine confides that 'poetry, the reading and the writing of it, has saved my life.": Maureen Doallas (Accessed online at *Tweetspeak Poetry*, "Interview With Poet Patty Paine (part 2): Poetry Can Save You," May 2014). http://www.tweet speakpoetry.com/2014/05/09/interview-poet-patty-paine-part-2-poetry-can-save/

page 20   "askeered" and "poetry demons." Nancy Franson, Facebook, March 27, 2014.

Chapter 3

page 28   "poetry & pain." Ann Kroeker, personal correspondence, August 12, 2014.

page 30-31   "And this is very important to remember when reading or writing or painting or talking or whatever...": John Green. (Accessed online at John Green Books, "Questions about *Paper Towns*, Q: Where did the strings metaphor come from?"). http://johngreenbooks.com/pt-questions/#process

page 31   "It's annoying and I don't understand it..." Monica Beeson McNeil, Facebook, May 27, 2014.

page 33   "#fightbackwithyellow," Nancy Franson, Facebook, March 7, 2015.

Chapter 4

page 35   "Fifteen minutes in she knew she had done this before...": Clif Drummond, personal correspondence, April 17, 2015.

page 36   "Back; forward; back; forward; release...": Seth Haines (Accessed online at *Tweetspeak Poetry*, "Become a Better Writer:

Fly Fishing Artist Date," June 2014). http://www.tweet speakpoetry.com/2014/06/06/fly-fishing-artist-date/

page 37   "I suspect that my comments about being afraid of poetry had something to do with it…": Nancy Franson, personal correspondence, April 1, 2014.

Chapter 6
page 54   "I've wasted a lot of time not reading Neruda,": Clif Drummond, personal interview, July 14, 2014.

Chapter 7
page 60   The Cancer Poetry Project, (Accessed online at YouTube.) https://www.youtube.com/channel/UCWcKe54S0uSF6WES hmJzTxQ

page 66-68   "When she was born, I started writing a journal to her…": Sally Clark, personal interview. March 6, 2014.

Chapter 8
page 69   "On Tuesday and Wednesday, May 26th & 27th, I was feeling anxious…": Merry Nell Drummond, personal correspondence., July 9, 2009.

page 72   "Joy is, in a way, sorrow's flower": Christian Wiman, *My Bright Abyss* (New York: Farrar, Straus & Giroux, 2013), Kindle edition.

page 76   "Hmmm…..I got lost in it. :(too sophisticated for me?…": Sally Clark, personal correspondence, April 7, 2015.

Chapter 9
page 79-82   "A lot of times people who aren't acclimated to poetry…": Ben Myers, personal interview, May 12, 2014.

page 82   "If you are a child, you might like these poems…": "All Good Slides Are Slippery," *Poetry*, Lemony Snicket. September 3, 2013. (Accessed online at www.poetryfoundation.org.) http://www.poetryfoundation.org/poetrymagazine/arti cle/246328

Chapter 10

page 90   "Poet's Choice by Linda Pastan," *The Washington Post*, by Ron Charles. (Accessed online February 23, 2010.) http://voices. washingtonpost.com/shortstack/2010/02/poets_choice_by_li nda_pastan.html

page 90   "As I Walked Out One Evening," W. H. Auden, *Another Time* (New York: Random House, 1940).

page 91   "Mercy," Kevin Young, *Book of Hours* (New York: Alfred A. Knopf, 2014) p. 20.

page 92-94   "I don't read much faster than I can read aloud...": Elizabeth Crook, personal interview, August 12, 2014.

Chapter 12

page 104   "Poet Natasha Trethewey, Hymning the Native Guard," *Fresh Air*: WHYY in Philadelphia, July 16, 2007. (Accessed online at NPR.org). http://www.npr.org/2007/07/16/12003278/ poet-natasha-trethewey-hymning-the-native-guard

page 105   *The Writer's Almanac*, American Public Media. (Accessed online at The Writer's Almanac, March 7, 2014). http://writers almanac.publicradio.org/index.php?date=2014/03/07)

Chapter 13

page 111   American Dipper (Accessed online at The Cornell Lab of Ornithology, American Dipper.) http://www.allabout birds.org/guide/American_Dipper/id

page 112   "Are you ready for some POETRY?...": Mark Osler. (Accessed online at *Osler's Razor*, "It's time for the 3rd Razor Bad High School Poetry Contest!!!!," January 18, 2013.) http://os lersrazor.blogspot.com/search?q=super+depressing

Chapter 14

page 117   "her appalling daughters...": Nancy Franson, Facebook, March 22, 2015.

page 118   "pied": *Webster's New World College Dictionary*. (Accessed online

at AP Stylebook, Webster's New World College Dictionary
Results) http://www.apstylebook.com/online/?do=entry&id
=56869&src=WEB

Chapter 15

page 124   "It's difficult to see when you're in the thick of a crisis…":
Glynn Young, *Poetry at Work* (Ossining, New York, T. S. Po-
etry Press, 2013), p. 80.

page 124   "I felt you in this poem.": Ann Kroeker, personal correspon-
dence, January 16, 2014.

page 127   "Disappearing Rio Grande," Colin McDonald and Erich
Schlegel, *Texas Tribune* (Austin, Texas, June 21, 2014-January
23, 2015). (Accessed online at www.TexasTribune.org)
http://riogrande.texastribune.org

Chapter 17

page 139   Leigh Dempsey, yoga class at Wellness Center, Hill Country
Memorial, Fredericksburg, Texas 2015.

page 140   "It was a wild card use, right?…": Anna Mitchael, personal
correspondence, September 16, 2014.

Chapter 18

page 144   "poetry scares me": Nancy Franson, Facebook, March 4,
2013.

page 144   "some pig," "terrific," "radiant," and "humble": E.B. White,
Charlotte's Web (New York, Scholastic Corporation, 1980). p.
77, 94, 114, 141.

page 145   "Guess what I'm reading…" Nancy Franson, personal corre-
spondence, July 11, 2013.

page 145   "It is not often that someone comes along…": E.B. White,
Charlotte's Web (New York, Scholastic Corporation, 1980), p.
184.

Permissions

All poems in this book are reprinted with permission or are within the public domain. We are grateful to the authors, editors, and publishers who have given us permission to include these poems.

L. L. Barkat, "4" from "Bird On the Mountain" and "Sara Teasdale," from *Love, Etc.: Poems of Love, Laughter, Longing & Loss*, T. S. Poetry Press, 2014. Reprinted with permission of T. S. Poetry Press.

Claire Bateman, "The Woman at the Stoplight." First appeared in *Every Day Poems* (January 2014). Reprinted with permission of author.

Laura Boggess, "On the Eve of Your Thirteenth Birthday, for Jeffrey." First appeared in *Every Day Poems* (March 2012). Reprinted with permission of author.

Harriet Brown, "Shell." First appeared in *Every Day Poems* (July 2014). Reprinted with permission of author.

Sally Clark, "Unattended," 2014. Reprinted with permission of author.

Susanna H. Davis, "St. Margaret's Chapel, Edinburgh," 2015. Reprinted with permission of author.

Todd Davis, "What Lives in the Wake of Our Sleep," from *In the Kingdom of the Ditch*, Michigan State University Press, 2013. Reprinted with permission of Michigan State University Press.

Kim Dower, "Bottled Water," from *Slice of Moon*, Red Hen Press, 2013. Reprinted with permission of Red Hen Press.

Dana Gioia, "New Year's," from *Interrogations at Noon*, Graywolf Press, 2001. Reprinted with permission of author.

Daniel Handler (aka Lemony Snicket), "All Good Slides Are Slippery," from *Poetry* (September 2013). Reprinted with permission of Charlotte Sheedy Literary Agency and author.

Kathleen Jamie, "The Dipper," from *The Tree House*, Picador, 2004. Copyright © Kathleen Jamie, 2004. Reprinted with permission of Macmillan Publishers.

Stuart Kestenbaum, "Prayer for Joy," from *Only Now*, Deerbrook Editions, 2014. Reprinted with permission of Deerbrook Editions.

Ann Kroeker, "Fragile," 2014. Reprinted with permission of author.

Karla Kuskin, "Write About a Radish" from *The Tree House*, Copyright © Karla Kuskin, 1975, 1980. Reprinted with permission of Scott Treimel NY.

Katherine E. McGhee, "Monsters." First appeared at KUT.org (April 2014). Reprinted with permission of author.

Stuart Mills, "In the Low Countries," from *Poetry* (September 2013). Reprinted with permission of Rosemary Mills and Luke Mills.

Ruth Mowry, "The earth's economy." First appeared in *Every Day Poems* (June 2014). Reprinted with permission of author.

Helena Nelson, "With My Mother, Missing the Train," from *Plot and Counterplot*, Shoestring Press, 2010. Reprinted with permission of Shoestring Press.

Alicia Ostriker, "The Dogs at Live Oak Beach, Santa Cruz," from *The Little Space: Poems Selected and New, 1968-1998*, University of Pittsburgh Press, 1998. Reprinted with permission of University of Pittsburgh Press.

Anne M. Doe Overstreet, "Mare Draws Her Lover Fishing at Dusk," from *Delicate Machinery Suspended: Poems*, T. S. Poetry Press, 2011. Reprinted with permission of T. S. Poetry Press.

Ann Patchett, from *This Is the Story of a Happy Marriage*, "Fact and Fiction," excerpt from page 156, HarperColllins Publishers, 2013. Reprinted with permission of HarperCollins Publishers.

Luci Shaw, "What to sing." First appeared in *Every Day Poems* (March 2014). Reprinted with permission of author.

Joyce Sutphen, "The Wordsworth Effect." First appeared at *The Writer's Almanac*, writersalmanac.org (September 2008). Reprinted with permission of author.

Natasha Trethewey, "Monument," from *Native Guard*, Copyright © Natasha Trethewey, 2006. Reprinted with permission of Houghton Mifflin Harcourt Publishing Company.

Megan Willome, "The cure for writer's block." First appeared in *Every Day Poems* (October 2011). Reprinted with permission of author.

Megan Willome, "S'more." First appeared in *The Cancer Poetry Project 2: more poems by cancer patients and those who love them*, edited by Karin B. Miller, Tasora Books, 2013. Reprinted with permission of author.

Megan Willome, "Still." First appeared in *God in the Yard: Spiritual Practice for the Rest of Us*, by L. L. Barkat, T. S. Poetry Press, 2010. Reprinted with permission of T. S. Poetry Press.

Megan Willome, "Who Am I?" First appeared in *Every Day Poems* (July 2011). Reprinted with permission of author.

Acknowledgements

Thank you, Galinda (Laura Barkat), for contacting me on January 1, 2014. Thank you, John, for everything. Thank you, Frio sisters, for always believing and always praying. Thank you, Mom, for saving all my poems, and Dad, for giving me permission to write what I needed to about Mom. Thank you, everyone who first read the poems about my mom on my blog and said nice things. To everyone I contacted to request permission to use something you had said or written for this book and then didn't end up using it, my sincere apologies.

"Traveling through the Dark" by William Stafford, *Traveling Through the Dark*, Harper (1962); "Mayakovsky" by Frank O'Hara, *Meditations in an Emergency*, Grove Press (1957); "For Those Who Think Young," *Mad Men* (TV series by Matthew Weiner) (2008); "Do Not Go Gentle Into That Good Night" by Dylan Thomas, *Botteghe Oscure* literary journal (1951); "Jabberwocky" and the Jabberwock, by Lewis Carroll, *Through the Looking-Glass*, Macmillan Publishers (1871); *A Series of Unfortunate Events* series by Daniel Handler, HarperCollins (1999-2006); "Blue Moon" by Richard Rodgers and Lorenz Hart, Metro-Goldwyn-Mayer (1934); *Lying Awake* by Mark Salzman, Vintage Books (2001); *A Wrinkle in Time* by Madeleine L'Engle, Farrar, Straus & Giroux (1963); *The Fault in Our Stars* by John Green, Dutton Books (2012); "There's a certain slant of light" by Emily Dickinson (1890); "Degrees of Gray in Philipsburg," by Richard Hugo, *The Lady in Kicking Horse Reservoir*, Carnegie-Mellon University Press (1973); "Sonnet 55," by William Shakespeare, *The Sonnets of Shakespeare*, Thomas Thorpe (1609); "Howl" by Allen Ginsberg, *Howl and Other Poems*, City Lights Books (1955); "The Love Song of J. Alfred Prufrock" by T. S. Eliot, *Poetry* (June 1915); "Thirteen Ways of Looking at a Blackbird" by Wallace Stevens, Harmonium, Knopf (1923); "Nothing Gold Can Stay," by Robert Frost, *Yale Review* (1923); *The Washington Post*, News Service and Syndicate; "The Red Wheelbarrow" (originally titled "XXII,"] by William Carlos Williams, *Spring and All*, Contact Publishing Company (1923); "Song of Myself" by Walt Whitman, *Leaves of Grass*, Walt Whitman (1855); *Looking for Alaska* by John Green, Dutton Juvenile (2005); *Eleanor & Park* by Rainbow Rowell, St. Martin's Press (2013); "I had been hungry all the years" by Emily Dickinson, Roberts Brothers (1890); *Macbeth* by William Shakespeare, John Heminges and Henry Condell (1623); *Monday, Monday* by Elizabeth Crook, Sarah Crichton Books (2014); *Salt Moon* by Noel Crook, Southern Illinois University Press (2015); *The Manageable Cold: Poems* by Timothy McBride, *TriQuarterly* literary magazine, Northwestern University Press (2010); *All the Silver Pennies* edited by Blanche Jennings Thompson, Macmillan Publishers (1967); *Pegasus* by G.T. Bards, The Crockett Company (1982); NPR, National Public Radio; Abilene Writer's Guild Annual Contest, Poetry Unrhymed (2015); *Brown Girl Dreaming* by Jaqueline Woodson, Nancy Paulson Books, the Penguin Group, (2014); "Stopping by Woods on a Snowy Evening" by Robert Frost, New Hampshire, Henry Holt (1923); "In Flanders Fields" by John McCrae, *Punch* (December 8, 1915); Race for the Cure, Susan G. Komen Race for the Cure; *Webster's New College World Dictionary*, Webster's New World (1999); *Cinderella* (movie by Kenneth Branagh) (2015); Cinderella, Prince Charming, The Walt Disney Company; "Pied Beauty" by Gerard Manley Hopkins, *Poems of Gerard Manley Hopkins*, Humphrey Milford (Oxford

University Press) (1918); "Up-Hill" by Christina Rossetti, *Goblin Market and Other Poems*, Macmillan Publishers (1862); *Romeo and Juliet* by William Shakespeare (1597); Big Bend National Park, National Park Service; *The Texas Tribune*; *Silver Linings Playbook* (movie by David O. Russell) (2012); *The Tale of Jemima Puddle-Duck* by Beatrix Potter, Frederick Warne & Co. (1908); *The Jungle Book* by Rudyard Kipling, Macmillan Publishers (1894); *The Jungle Book* (movie by Wolfgang Reitherman) (1967); The Walt Disney Company; "Seal Lullaby" by Rudyard Kipling, *The Jungle Book*, Macmillan Publishers (1894); Harry Potter, Platform 9 ¾, horcrux, and *Harry Potter* series by J.K. Rowling, Scholastic (1999-2009); Sharpwriter No. 2 pencil, Paper Mate; *Water Bugs and Dragonflies: Explaining Death to Young Children* by Doris Stickney, The Pilgrim Press (1982); *Our Town* by Thornton Wilder (1938); *Fun Home* by Alison Bechdel, Mariner Books (2006); "Ring of Keys" by Lisa Kron and Jeanine Tesori, *Fun Home* (2013); "Half Mexican" by Juan Felipe Herrera, *Notes on the Assemblage*, City Lights Publishers (2015);"Choose Your Own Adventure" by Anna Mitchael, *Wacoan* (October 2014); "Extraordinary" by Megan Willome, *Wacoan* (April 2013); Templeton, Fern, Henry Fussy, Joy from *Charlotte's Web* by E.B. White, Harper & Brothers, (1952); *The Elements of Style* by William Strunk, Jr. and E.B. White, Harcourt, Brace & Howe (1920); *The New Yorker*, Condé Nast; *E.B. White on Dogs* by E.B. White, edited by Martha White, Tilbury House, Publishers (2013); "Death of a Pig" by E.B. White, *Atlantic Monthly* (January 1948); Moleskine is a registered trademark of Moleskine SpA; *Texas Monthly*, Emmis Publishing, LP; "Maybe we first met this arching dome" by Naomi Shihab Nye, "Big Bend 2015," *Texas Monthly* (May 2015); "The Mercy" by Philip Levine, *The Mercy,* Knopf (2000); "Thanatopsis" by William Cullen Bryant, H. Altemus (1817); "The Raven" by Edgar Allan Poe, *The American Review* (1845); "When I Heard the Learn'd Astronomer" by Walt Whitman, *Drum-Taps*, Peter Eckler (1865); *Breaking Bad* (episode "Box Cutter," TV series by Vince Gilligan) (2011); Skype; Voxer.

Also from T. S. Poetry Press

How to Read a Poem: Based on the Billy Collins Poem "Introduction to Poetry," by Tania Runyan

Runyan's book reads like a playful love letter—a creative intercession on poetry's behalf—to the hearts of a new generation, those on whom so much, like the future of the art, depends.

—Brad Davis, Poet, teacher, and counselor at Pomfret School

On Being a Writer: 12 Simple Habits for a Writing Life that Lasts, by Ann Kroeker and Charity Singleton Craig

A genial marriage of practice and theory. For writers new and seasoned. This book is a winner.

—Philip Gulley, author of *Front Porch Tales*

Sun Shine Down, by Gillian Marchenko

From the very first page, Marchenko tugs the heartstrings of anyone who has ever experienced—or wanted to experience—parenthood, leaving us with a broadened view of the universe and a deeper understanding of what it really means to love one another.

—Julie Cantrell, *New York Times* and *USA Today* bestselling author

Masters in Fine Living Series

The Masters in Fine Living Series is designed to help people
live a whole life through the power of reading, writing,
and just plain living. Look for titles with the tabs **read, write,
live, play, learn,** or **grow**—and join a culture of individuals
interested in living deeply, richly.

T. S. Poetry Press titles are available online in e-book and print
editions. Print editions also available through Ingram.

tspoetry.com